A BULGAKOV ANTHOLOGY

SERGIUS BULGAKOV

A Bulgakov Anthology

Edited by
James Pain and Nicolas Zernov

WIPF & STOCK · Eugene, Oregon

Wipf and Stock Publishers
199 W 8th Ave, Suite 3
Eugene, OR 97401

Sergius Bulgakov
A Bulgakov Anthology
By Bulgakov, Sergius and Zernov, Nicolas
Copyright©1976 SPCK
ISBN 13: 978-1-49826-465-5
Publication date 7/15/2012
Previously published by SPCK, 1976

The thanks of the editors and the publisher are due to the
Y.M.C.A. Press, 11 rue de la Montagne-Ste-Geneviève,
Paris, who control the rights in Sergius Bulgakov's work
in the original language.

Thanks are also due to William Heinemann Ltd and the
Macmillan Publishing Company Inc., New York, for per-
mission to reproduce copyright material from *The Brothers
Karamazov* by Fyodor M. Dostoyevsky, translated by
Constance Garnett (London 1912; New York 1950).

Contents

vi   *Contents*

7   *An American Sermon: 1934*

8   *Festival Sermons*

Preface

Sergius Nicolaevich Bulgakov, born in 1871, Professor of Political Economy in Moscow University, ordained to the priesthood in 1923, who died in Paris in 1944 as Dean of the Russian Orthodox Theological Academy there, was one of the most original and gifted theologians of the Russian Church. He belonged to that group of Russian intellectuals who converted from Marxism to Christian Orthodoxy on the eve of the fall of the Russian Empire.

This Anthology is published in the hope that English-speaking readers may find an introduction to the thought of Father Bulgakov, whose ideas would otherwise remain largely inaccessible to them. The texts have been rendered into English by the late Mrs Natalie Duddington and Professor James Pain; and the work has been edited by Dr Pain in co-operation with Dr Nicolas Zernov. The late Professor Lev Zander, well-known authority on the thought of Father Bulgakov, has provided a *Memoir* in which he indicates his place in Russian theology.

Introduction

Since the turn of this century ecumenical developments between the Eastern and Western Christians have advanced in so dramatic a manner as to obscure something of the intensity with which previous generations had fostered separation and division among the churches. The present open, friendly discourse which we enjoy may appear so natural and reasonable that we tend to forget the long years of polemicism and suspicion which have characterized much of Christian history.

In the case of the Russian Church the theological factors in separation were bolstered by geographical and cultural isolation. The Church of Russia was self-contained for centuries, set apart linguistically, and thus was little known even by other Orthodox churchmen. It was not until the ·mid-seventeenth century that the Russians became concerned with identifying the Greek and Latin traditions as such. And this development led to tragic division among the Russians themselves.

Subsequently, the eighteenth-century Church reforms of Peter the Great tended to focus upon Orthodox theology as the negation of both Roman Catholicism and Protestantism. Rather than the formulation of constructive theology, this period saw the emergence of a curious scholasticism largely concerned to clarify what the Orthodox did *not* believe. Russian theology was therefore driven into even greater separation because of its self-defensive posture.

The nineteenth century saw a turning point with the work of the Russian lay theologian Alexei S. Khomiakov (1804–60). Indeed, modern Russian theology dates from his efforts, however disputed, to advance a positive Orthodox position which was not simply based upon the refutation of Roman Catholic and Protestant theological claims. He also inaugurated an unofficial ecumenical discourse by publishing a number of

Introduction

theological essays in Western Europe[1] and by his extended correspondence with an Englishman, William Palmer of Magdalen College, Oxford.[2] Today Khomiakov is best remembered for his ecclesiology; specifically for his concept of the organic unity of the Church which is identified with the term 'sobornost'. His understanding of catholicity has provided a great stimulus to later Russian theologians.

From a very different point of view the work of another theologian, Vladimir S. Solovyov (1853–1900) has coloured twentieth-century Russian theology. He advanced the cause of Church union in a prophetic manner. He also contributed significantly to the recovery of Christian Platonism in the Russian Church; to an awakened concern for the understanding of God-manhood; and to the emergence of modern sophiology.[3]

Father Sergius Bulgakov stood in this line of modern Russian theology dating from the early nineteenth century. He built upon Khomiakov's ecclesiology, Solovyov's sophiology, and Fyodor Dostoyevsky's penetrating vision of freedom. Yet he also brought to his work as a theologian and ecumenist a distinctive contribution of his own. As an ex-Marxist he understood as few have done the oddly western character of Marxism. In turning from Marxism to Christian Orthodoxy he was able to discern the roots of modern dialectical materialism in much older Christian heresy.

As in the nineteenth century Khomiakov analysed the Roman Catholic–Protestant schism from the point of view of Orthodoxy, so now Bulgakov approached the question of dialogue between Christians and Marxists from the same vantage point. Moved in part by an acute sense of urgency surrounding the confrontation with Marxism, Father Bulgakov took bold initiative in his contacts with Western Christians. In this he was very much on his own. His Orthodox brethren tended to remain aloof and to limit their ecumenical participation to defensive rejoinder. Bulgakov offered many

---

[1] Khomiakov, A. S., *L'Eglise Latine et le Protestantisme au point de vue de l'Eglise d'Orient* (Lausanne, 1872).

[2] Birkbeck, W. J., *Russia and the English Church During the Last Fifty Years* (London, 1895).

[3] Zoubov, P. P., *Soloviev on Godmanhood* (Poughkeepsie, 1944).

ideas of his own in the early days of the ecumenical movement.

He had deep insight into the potential of Divine Grace in moving towards the reintegration of the Church. In this light he proposed partial intercommunion, based not upon an appeal to some 'lowest common denominator' of Christian affirmation, but upon a sound agreement with regard to the fundamentals of the gospel jointly professed in an act of repentance. This suggestion he embodied in a highly controversial document published in 1933 which called for partial intercommunion as a means of Anglican-Orthodox reconciliation.

In this and in other matters he showed a dislike for the tendency to talk only of our agreements and to maintain silence upon points of serious difference. At the Faith and Order Conference of 1927 in Lausanne he startled many of the Protestants present by presenting a statement concerning the veneration due the Blessed Virgin Mary, Theotokos. Though they were not in agreement with him, they admired his honest, straightforward manner.

Father Bulgakov did not run away from conflict and argument if he felt that some good could come from engaging in it. Nicolas Zernov has written of him that 'he was a fighter; a singularly fearless man who had no hesitation in making himself unpopular by raising questions which others would have preferred to shelve'.[1]

Now, after half a century of ecumenical organization, a new generation of Christians is rising among whom the old vision of ecumenism appears to have lost its charm. To some the quest for Christian unity seems to have been betrayed by ecclesiastical bureaucracy. Others are calling for a return to the fundamentals of the gospel and for submission to the Holy Spirit as a basis for charismatic renewal. And throughout the Christian world there is a demand for candour, coupled with a sense of urgency inspired by the signs of the times.

It is with a peculiar cogency that Father Bulgakov speaks to the present situation. His dislike of superficiality, his insistence that Christians must get down to basics in their

[1] Zernov, N. M., *The Russian Religious Renaissance of the Twentieth Century* (London, 1963), p. 143.

conversations with one another, his probing analysis of
Marxism, his reliance upon the Grace of God, and his faithful
expectation of the Parousia all commend him to contemporary
readers. He was clearly a man ahead of his time, a pioneer in
spiritual matters. He anticipated by more than thirty years
many of the considerations of Vatican II.

Sergius Bulgakov was by nature deeply and distinctively
Russian. He traced his family history to a Tartar named
Bulgak, who was converted from Islam to Orthodox Christianity during the Russo-Mongolian struggle of the sixteenth
century. Bulgakov himself represented the seventh generation
of priests and deacons in his family.

He was born on 16 July 1871 in the central Russian town of
Livny, where he was raised in the colourful atmosphere of
Orthodox faith and culture. But at the age of twelve he
rebelled against the strictures of life in a Church school. By
the time he was fourteen he had determined against a career in
the Church and thought of himself as a revolutionary nihilist.
For fifteen years he associated with the Marxist intelligentsia.
During these formative years he completed his formal education, studied in Moscow, Berlin, Paris, and London, and
published his first major book: *The Role of the Market in
Capitalist Production.*

In 1898 he married Elena Ivanovna Tokmakova. His
marriage was a happy one, and some of the deepest moments
of his religious experience in subsequent years were set in the
context of his family life. He had three sons and one daughter.
When his three-year-old son Ivan died in 1909, he wrote: 'In
the light of a new, hitherto completely unknown experience
heavenly joy together with the pain of crucifixion descended
into my heart, and in the darkness of God-forsakenness, God
reigned in my soul.'[1]

In 1901, Bulgakov published two volumes entitled *Capitalism and Agriculture.* In this study he evidenced far less conviction in Marxism than he did in his earlier work on the *Role
of the Market.* By the turn of the century he was a man disillusioned by the religion of progress and disenchanted by the
glamour of the West. His thinking turned from German philosophy to Russian spirituality. On 21 November 1901, he gave

[1] Bulgakov, S. N., *Avtobiographicheskie zametki* (Paris, 1946), p. 68.

a public lecture on Dostoyevsky, in Kiev. Much to his surprise, his address was received with tremendous enthusiasm by a crowd of students, who gave him a standing ovation. This event was to mark a turning point in his career.

From 1901 to 1906, he occupied the chair of Political Economy at Kiev Polytechnic Institute. He was well received by the students and soon became a leader of the young movement of religious intelligentsia. In 1903 his book *From Marxism to Idealism* came out. This collection of essays shows the influence of Dostoyevsky upon his thinking. In 1906 he was appointed professor of Political Economy at Moscow University Institute of Commerce. In the decade following his move to Moscow, he wrote a great number of articles, essays, and studies in political theory. (His *History of Political and Economic Theory* serves to illustrate his scope and competence as a theoretician.) In 1909 he joined with Nicolas Berdyaev, Simeon Frank, and others in the publication of a significant symposium on the Russian intelligentsia, entitled *Signposts*.

However, Sergius Bulgakov was no ordinary political scientist. In 1912 he wrote an unusual volume which bore the prosaic title *Philosophy of Economics*. It was in this work that he gave his first systematic statement on sophiology—the unifying concept in his philosophy. He was concerned to develop a world-view consistent with historic Orthodoxy which would prove adequate to meet the challenge of technology and modern science. Great controversy has been aroused by his contention that the world is a manifestation of Sophia, the Divine Wisdom. Some of the Orthodox condemn the notion as non-Christian gnosticism, while others find that Bulgakov has succeeded in structuring his system in such a way as to render it compatible with traditional theology.[1] (A further development of the idea came in his *Unfading Light*, published in 1917.)

During his career at Moscow University he was active in political, social, and philosophical circles. In 1907 and 1908 he was a member of the Second Duma. As such he campaigned against capital punishment and became well informed on

---

[1] The most complete discussion available on the question is to be found in the excellent study of Bulgakov's theology by Lev Zander, entitled *Bog i Mir* (Paris, 1948).

national issues. Many of his lectures, tracts, and articles written prior to the Communist Revolution have been published in two collections. The first of these appeared in 1911 under the title *Two Cities*; this was followed in 1918 by *Quiet Thoughts*. The essays cover a wide range of subject matter, from art criticism to apocalyptic vision.

In 1917 he was made a professor at the University of Moscow and was appointed as a delegate to the All-Russian Church Sobor. It was this Sobor which acted to restore the Patriarch of Moscow. (From the time of Peter the Great the Moscow Patriarchate had been governed by a Holy Synod.) Bulgakov was elected as one of two laymen on the new Patriarch's advisory council.

By 1918, Bulgakov's pilgrimage from Marxism to idealism had led him to deep involvement in the life of the Church. However, he maintained his University post until after his ordination as a priest in June of that year. The Communists then expelled him from the University, and his position became quite difficult. (He recounts that on one occasion Prince E. N. Trubetskoy phoned him late at night to warn him in Latin of his impending arrest.) His career in Russia ended with a period as lecturer at Simferopol University in the Crimea. He was exiled from the U.S.S.R. on 1 January 1923.

During the difficult years at Simferopol, Father Bulgakov continued to lecture and write. When he was forced to leave Russia he took with him two major manuscripts which represent his work in the Crimea. One of these, *The Tragedy of Philosophy*, was published in Germany in 1927. The other work, *Philosophical Introduction to the Veneration of the Name of God*, was printed in France after his death.

As a refugee he first landed at Constantinople. An account of his visit to Hagia Sophia is included in this volume. Though he had lost his possessions and his homeland he maintained a sense of enthusiasm and expectation which characterized his theological perspective for the rest of his life. From Constantinople he went to Prague, then the centre of the Russian émigré community. The mid-twenties were the golden years of the émigrés. They were a hopeful and confident company. Everyone looked for the imminent liberation of Russia from

Communist tyranny. Their vision was of a promised land, freed from autocracy and open to the development of a transformed society. The Russian Student Christian Movement was born of this enthusiasm, and Father Bulgakov was instrumental in forming the life of the Movement. Prior to the Revolution the Orthodox had looked upon the S.C.M. and related movements from a distance, for they were identified as 'Protestant' agencies. The new Movement was to take on a distinctively Orthodox nature, though its membership was inclusive. From the beginning of the life of the Movement, Father Bulgakov encouraged conferees to consider the Eucharist as the centre of their society. In this way the R.S.C.M. took on a distinctive character which contributed greatly to the depth of its activities in following years.

In addition to his work with the R.S.C.M., Father Bulgakov served as lecturer in the Russian Law Institute which had been opened by émigrés in Prague. He continued to study theology and wrote a number of doctrinal essays. In 1925 it was decided that a Russian Orthodox Theological Academy should be founded in Paris. Metropolitan Eulogius invited Father Bulgakov to come as professor of dogmatics and dean of the new school. His acceptance of the position brought him to Paris and inaugurated the last, most creative period of his life.

During his Paris years he continued active in the R.S.C.M. and was one of the founders of the Fellowship of St Alban and St Sergius at High Leigh in 1927. He participated in the Ecumenical Conferences at Lausanne, Oxford, and Edinburgh, and was active in the work of the Continuing Committee on Faith and Order. In 1934 he made an extensive tour of the United States and Canada, at the invitation of the Protestant Episcopal Church.

Father Bulgakov's life was centred around the Chapel at the Theological Academy. His day began there at seven o'clock with the celebration of the Divine Liturgy and ended late at night following Vespers. Along with his teaching and and administrative work he maintained a full schedule of preaching and pastoral care in addition to his study and writing.

During his tenure in Paris he wrote two trilogies. The first of these includes *The Burning Bush* (1927), *The Friend of the Bridegroom* (1927), and *Jacob's Ladder* (1929). These works deal with the Mother of God, John the Baptist, and the Holy Angels, though their common theme is the Divine Wisdom in the created world. The second trilogy has as its theme God-manhood. It consists of *The Lamb of God* (1988), *The Comforter* (1936), and *The Bride of the Lamb* (1945). The last of these and *The Johannine Apocalypse* (1948) were both published after his death. His later theological works met with severe criticism and occasional hostility in Orthodox circles. Controversy is still alive concerning his sophiology. Fortunately, the bishops of the Western European metropolitanate gave their full canonical support to the maintenance of his freedom as a theologian.

In 1989 Father Bulgakov was stricken with cancer of the throat. As a result he was faced with two major operations and the loss of his vocal chords. The magnitude of his spirit is revealed in his autobiographical notes concerning these experiences. He learned to speak 'without a voice' and was able to continue to celebrate the early morning Liturgy. During the years of war which marked his final illness he developed further the eschatological expectation which had come to characterize his faith. His last book, on the *Apocalypse*, is far from an ordinary commentary. It is a remarkable testimony of one whose insight was coloured by a deep personal expectation of the coming of his Lord. His favourite, constant prayer was 'Even so, come, Lord Jesus.'

On Whit Monday in 1944 (the twenty-sixth anniversary of his ordination), Father Bulgakov celebrated his last Liturgy. He was found unconscious that night and died forty days later, on 12 July. At his funeral the Metropolitan Eulogius addressed him:

Dear Father Sergius: You were a Christian sage, a teacher of the Church in the purest and most lofty sense. You were enlightened by the Holy Spirit, the Spirit of Wisdom, the Spirit of Understanding, the Comforter to Whom you dedicated your scholarly work. He transformed the Saul in you into Paul. He guided you to your last breath. Twenty-six years ago you partook of His gracious gifts in the sacrament of ordination, and you bore the cross of priesthood in the Holy Spirit. It is significant that you received this gift on the day of the Holy Spirit—when He descended upon the holy apostles in tongues of fire. Thus you had a share in them. You were an apostle in your life ... It is significant, too, that you celebrated your last Liturgy on earth on that very day of the Holy Spirit, the anniversary of your ordination as a priest . . . How bright your countenance was on that day! Your soul was conscious of its last triumph in this world. And it was on that day that the Lord called you to cease your priestly service on earth so as to continue it there, at the throne of God, in the choir of holy Angels and Apostles.

JAMES PAIN

Memoir

In the history of Russian thought there are several men whose life and work reflect Russia as a whole. Their thought not merely sums up the past but throws light upon the future, and therefore we should not only study it but learn from it. One such is Father Sergius Bulgakov. The present anthology is intended as a stepping-stone to the discovery of his creative and original thought. The editors have selected from the treasury of Father Sergius' writings pages that seemed to them particularly significant and characteristic, and thus likely to give the reader some idea both of his range of thought and of his personality. But of course, a more thorough grasp of his philosophy and theology requires acquaintance with his works in full; extracts can merely serve as an introduction to the study of them.

In the course of his evolution Father Sergius travelled a long way from Marxism to Orthodoxy and priesthood. Various aspects of philosophical idealism marked the intermediate stages of his course, and the different temptations that beset him were obstacles on the way: the temptation of scepticism after his disappointment with Marxism; of abstract scholarship at the period of his preoccupation with philosophy; of liberal Christianity after his conversion to religion; of the invincibility of Rome after the disintegration of Russia. Father Sergius was not alone on that path—many Russian thinkers had followed it. But almost all of them journeyed only a part of the way, bequeathing the rest of it to future generations. Father Sergius was far in advance of his time, and his life and thought mapped out a programme which we feel to be a call but can neither fully grasp nor still less carry out.

There was another peculiarity about his spiritual development which imparts a unique value to it. In passing from one stage to another he never confined himself merely to rejecting the past. He singled out all the positive elements in it, including them in a sublimated and transfigured form in the next

and higher stage of thought. Thus, having overcome materialism Father Sergius did not replace it, as many do, by a one-
sided spiritualism but took matter to be the basis of the divine
world, essential for the very possibility of the Incarnation. In
this way he brought matter into his sophiological scheme and
then into the Chalcedonian synthesis. The same applies to his
rejection of Marxism: all its positive features are taken into
account and incorporated in the *Philosophy of Economics*, in
consequence of which the book is the best antidote to Marxism.
His break with Kantianism did not mean a disregard of
intellectual honesty and of moral earnestness; the break with
liberal theology involved the rejection of its claim to replace
faith by reason and of its groundless negations, but certainly
not of its insistence upon responsible critical thinking.

In consequence, Father Sergius' past always lived in his
present. He was uncompromisingly hostile to 'intellectualism',
but he remained an authority and a spirtual guide for the
'intellectuals'. They all found that at some stage of his
development he had lived through the same doubts and
strivings as they did, so that he could not only understand
them from within but also interpret their own minds to them
and point out their spiritual path. The seeking and the
doubting found in him a physician and not a judge: he never
passed sentence on anyone, but diagnosed, gave advice,
pointed out the way, called to higher things. This is equally
true of his learned articles and of his sermons, talks, and
counsel to penitents.

Another characteristic of his thought was that he always
treated his intellectual opponents fairly and did not assume
that they were stupid or dishonest. In religious debates and
apologetics we often simplify our task by slandering our
opponents—deliberately or unconsciously—and picturing
them as rationally deficient. To feel and recognize the strength
of one's adversary requires much courage, open-mindedness,
and honesty; it seems to weaken our chances of victory, but
on the other hand it renders our arguments far more convincing and valuable. Father Sergius' articles on Feuerbach,
Marx, Robert Owen, Picasso, and Rudolf Steiner are sufficient
to show how attentively he followed the thought of minds
alien to his own and how he could learn from his opponents,

not merely rejecting their errors but finding a proper place for them in the general dialectic of philosophical and theological problems.

The first critical task for Father Sergius' thought was to overcome Marxism; he did so along three different lines. (1) The attempt to interpret the problems of agriculture in Marxist categories showed him the limitations of the theory and its inapplicability to this particular branch of economics. That was a criticism of Marxism from within. (2) Epistemological analysis of Marxist thought brought to light the unproved and arbitrary nature of its dogmatic assumptions. Kant's critique, which had once shown that a materialistic metaphysic was impossible, proved fatal to Marxist dialectic also. (8) A careful study of Marxism as a philosophy (and not merely as an economic doctrine) detected in it a surreptitiously introduced anthropology and metaphysic which were accepted as axioms, without any ground or proof.

These were the signposts of the path from Marxism to 'idealism'. By idealism was meant both Kant's critical philosophy and the primacy of the spiritual principle, characteristic of the great systems of German idealism and of the religious thought of Christian philosophers. Thus critical philosophy proved to lead to Christian thought.

The path from abstract idealism to a Christian sophiology was more difficult. It involved overcoming the epistemological barrenness of Kant and the neo-Kantians (all Russian philosophers of the end of the nineteenth and the beginning of the twentieth century have had to grapple with this problem). It also meant taking into account the essential truth contained in Fichte's and Hegel's arguments. Father Sergius carried out the first task in *The Philosophy of the Name* and the second in *The Tragedy of Philosophy*. On close inspection all these systems of thought appeared to him as different aspects of a trinitarian heresy. They one-sidedly affirmed the principles of (1) personal being (Fichte's absolute ego), (2) ideal content (Hegel's pan-logism), and (8) vital self-determination (the spiritualism of the Roman School). Such an interpretation enabled him to overcome their one-sidedness and include their positive attainments in a system of Christian philosophy.

The next critical task before Father Sergius was to dispose

of his internal religious temptations. He dealt with liberalism in his article 'Modern Arianism—a Professors' Religion' and provided a spiritual diagnosis of 'scientific' Christianity which 'substitutes a University seminar for the experience of spiritual life and puts theologians in the place of saints'. The attraction to Roman Catholicism (discussed in his unpublished dialogue _By the Walls of the Chersonese_) led him to examine critically Catholic dogmas of the Immaculate Conception and of Papal Infallibility. This was the starting point of his work as a theologian.

Such is the general outline of Father Sergius' critical work. Having cleared the ground, he built upon it a grand edifice of constructive thought, a kind of philosophical and theological _Summa_. It is characterized by the fact that it has no separate and independent parts, but everything in it is penetrated by the same spirit and starts from the same point, to which it eventually returns.

It would not be possible to give here a full exposition of Father Sergius' system of thought;[1] only its main features can be briefly outlined. Indeed, it was not his intention to create a 'system'. God's world was for him a mystery which eludes the grasp of reason and cannot be forced into the framework of limited human thought. But a mystery is not a secret deliberately hidden from man. It is never wholly accessible to him because it transcends his intellectual powers, but as these powers increase he may apprehend it in part, though he cannot hope to master it completely. Accordingly, in philosophy as well as in theology it is the starting point that is essential— the direction which our thought follows and not this or that section of the path traversed by it. The important thing is the idea which guides us along the thorny paths of knowledge. The attempts to grasp and systematize our discoveries on the way can never be wholly successful.

The leading idea of Father Sergius' thought was that of _revelation_: that everything is a revelation of God—of his wisdom, power, and glory. Theology tells us that the Father reveals himself in the Son and in the Spirit—begetting the Son and giving procession to the Holy Spirit while remaining

---

[1] I have done this in my book _Bog i Mir: Mirosozertsanie O. C. Bulgakova_ (Paris, 1948).

in substantial unity with them. The Holy Trinity as the revelation of the Father is the basic theme of Christian theology. Philosophy tells us of how the Creator (God the Father) reveals himself in creation, manifesting his wisdom through the Son by whom the world is made, and his glory through the life-giving Spirit. The world as the revelation of the Creator is the basic theme of Christian philosophy. Thus philosophy re-echoes the theme of theology, forming a unity with it 'without division or confusion'. Their common *motif* is the idea that everything is a revelation of God and bears his stamp. This primary nearness between the Creator and the creature lies at the basis of Father Sergius' conception of man and of the world. It is fully developed in the doctrine of God-manhood which is the presupposition of Christology and of the doctrines of the Holy Spirit, of the Church, and of the 'last things'. All things prove to be interconnected; philosophy and theology are not separate disciplines but parts of one and the same wisdom, of the same apprehension of Sophia, manifested to us in creation and in the Scriptures, in nature and in the Church. Hence, true love of wisdom, true philo-Sophia must take everything into account: it cannot be based upon any particular set of facts but has to reckon with the fullness of God's revelation in the world. With regard to theology this means that the source of theological ideas is not Scripture only, but Church life as a whole, with all its dogmatic, liturgical, and iconographic content. In science and philosophy our reason must not be confined to the narrow framework of sensuous experience or to the laws of logic, but must co-ordinate its data with the revelations of religion and the intuitions of art.

This is Father Sergius' main idea. He made many different attempts to work it out and to formulate in philosophical and theological terms the truth that had been revealed to him. There is no absolute unity or consistency in these attempts: he was tentative, always progressing and seeking a new approach. He used to say that some parts of his work were carved in marble and others made of cardboard. The first is unquestionably true of his basic standpoint; the second applies to his different attempts to express it as a doctrine.

Broadly speaking, he has two doctrinal formulations of

sophiology. In *The Unfading Light* and the books immediately following it, Father Sergius develops the idea of the cosmic Sophia as the intelligible basis of the world. The force of his contention is that the world's noumenal ground, whatever name we may give to it, is not simply a 'thing in itself' but belongs to God, is divine wisdom, and cannot be apprehended apart from God. True philosophy thus proves to be a Christian philosophy, and everything temporal finds its value, meaning, and significance in the light of eternity. But although the world is conceived as God's world, its existence is not shown to involve the deeper truths of the Christian dogma. When Father Sergius entered upon a special study of theology he came to the conclusion that he must interpret his sophiology in the categories of doctrinal thought. The problem of the relation between God and the world now appeared to him as that of the relation between the divine and the human natures in the Person of Christ. The Chalcedonian dogma provided the key to sophiology. But the Chalcedonian formula merely contains four negative propositions and tells us how *not* to think of the relation between the divine and the human natures in Christ. The positive meaning of the formula, the Chalcedonian *yea* is, according to Father Sergius, the bequest of the Patristic age to future generations, and it is our duty to work at it. And so he devoted all his further theological writings to this task. In his own words, he set out to formulate the doctrine of God-manhood and the inner unity between the divine and the created Sophia. At this stage his mind was already enriched by the dogmatic teaching of the Church, and he was developing his theory of Sophia in its theological and not in its cosmological aspect. Hence his books of that period speak no longer of the world and of man, but of the Father, of Christ, of the Holy Spirit, of Our Lady, of St John the Baptist, and of the angels; of the Church and its destiny in the world; and of the End. But it is all interconnected; the book about Christ is a grandeur of Christian metaphysics; the book about the Holy Spirit contains implicitly a teaching about the nature of life and creativity; the book about the Mother of God lays the foundations of a Christian philosophy of cosmos; the book about John the Baptist is an essay in Christian anthropology.

The main characteristic of Father Sergius' thought is its inner unity: all things in it are bound up with everything else. And yet it cannot be called a system, for its separate parts are not interconnected in the order of logical sequence or deduced from one central idea. Father Sergius' speculation has for its starting point the data of revelation, of human life as a whole, of nature, and of art; it thus includes facts which appear to be totally disconnected. In striving to find a principle which would weld them into a single whole Father Sergius arrives at a unique kind of synthesis. It provides true spiritual food for the modern mind, torn asunder by the struggle between conflicting disciplines, tendencies, and aims. The disease of our time is the loss of the sense of unity between consciousness and life, the opposition between religion and philosophy, philosophy and science, science and art, art and morality. Father Sergius' thought, like a ray of light proceeding from a single point but extending to every domain of life, shows a true path to the reinstatement in mankind of 'the mind of Christ' in whom there is 'not yea and nay, but in Him is yea, for all the promises of God in Him are yea, and in Him Amen'.[1]

LEV ZANDER

1

Autobiographical Notes

The essays which follow were written at various times in Bulgakov's life and published after his death (*Avtobiographicheskie Zametki*, Paris, 1946). The essay on Hagia Sophia appears in Zander, L. A., *Pamyati O. Sergiya Bulgakova* (Paris, 1945).

Autobiographical Notes

I was born in a priest's family, and Levite blood of six generations flowed in my veins. I grew up near the parish church of St Sergius, in the gracious atmosphere of its prayers and within the sound of its bells. The aesthetic, moral, and everyday recollections of my childhood are bound up with the life of that parish church. Within its walls my heart rejoiced in prayer and mourned the departed. Until I was an adolescent I was faithful to my birth and upbringing as a son of the Church. I attended the parochial school in my native town, Livny, for four years and was then sent to the Theological Seminary in Oryol for three years.

In early adolescence, during my first or second year at the Seminary, I went through a religious crisis—painful but not tragic—which ended in my losing religious faith for many, many years. From the age of fourteen to about thirty the prodigal son withdrew into a far country to the sorrow and dismay of many, principally of his parents. I had a great deal to lose, and I gave it up with seeming ease, without any struggle (though in my godlessness I did think of suicide).

The initial impulse for my revolt came apparently from childish vanity: I had been praised too much at school and was all the more keenly stung by the rudeness which prevailed at the Seminary. But that was superficial. Far more important were youthful doubts and questions which there was no one to answer. They were increased by external influences and meeting with people, but above all by the typical mentality of the 'intelligentsia'. I became a victim of it both personally and historically, together with my innumerable Russian brethren. It was the general fate of humanistic mankind, which we have yet to outlive: the temptation to worship man.

My revolt against my surroundings was morally right in so far as it was inspired by love of freedom and disgust at the servility which then reigned in the clerical world (and at that time it was the only world I knew). I did not want to be reconciled to it, indeed I could not be, and it would not have been right. I fled from it to save my spiritual integrity, and to this day I consider my flight justified.

In losing religious faith I naturally and, as it were, automatically adopted the revolutionary mood then prevalent among the intelligentsia. Without belonging to any particular party, I was bitterly opposed to the monarchism which was dominant in our clerical circles. In short, at that period in my life I went through the same experience as my predecessors in the Seminaries (Chernyshevsky, Dobrolyubov, and others). I fell victim to a gloomy revolutionary nihilism, though in my case it was always combined with a love of art and literature which saved me. The general atmosphere of the theological schools, based on tradition and compulsion, was impotent to combat this nihilism and grew more and more unendurable to a proud and independent boy who genuinely loved truth and freedom.

The Seminary authorities intended me for the Theological Academy, but I felt that my only hope of salvation was to escape from the Seminary at once, without looking back. Where might I escape? 'To be useful', to serve mankind and progress by scientific thought—towards which I always had a leaning. It was not easy for me to carry out my plan. It demanded sacrifices, not only from me but from my family, and in the first place from my parents (whom, in my youthful egoism, I considered least of all). Nevertheless, in the summer of 1888 I left the Oryol Seminary. After attending the classical school at Yalets for two years, I entered Moscow University as a student in the Faculty of Law in the autumn of 1890.

In my choice of faculty I followed the herd of the intelligentsia against my personal inclination. I was attracted by philology, philosophy, and literature, but chose law, which did not appeal to me. I did this with the idea that I might help save my country from Tsarist tyranny. And to this end I had to take up the social sciences and bind myself to political economy like a galley slave chained to his bench. I doomed myself voluntarily to go through this purgatory that I might redeem my sin as a prodigal son.

I entered the University with the firm intention of devoting myself to a discipline alien to me, and I carried out my decision. After graduation I was called by Moscow University to be a lecturer in political economy. My appointment was made by Professor A. I. Chuprov, the kindest and nicest man imaginable, whose fate was similar to mine: he too had been a theological student and recalled his past as a lost paradise, but he was not destined to reach the promised land beyond the 'intellectualistic wilderness'. I can well fancy how perturbed he would have been at seeing me in a cassock; but he did not live to see such a shocking thing.

My mind developed along the lines of social and socialistic thought. Consecutively, and almost automatically, I then passed from one form of thought to another until finally I appeared enslaved by Marxism, which suited me about as well as a saddle fits a cow. In the years 1898 to 1900 the University sent me to study abroad. Naturally, I went first to Germany—the land of Marxism and Social Democracy. But there, contrary to all my expectation, I soon met with disappointment, and my *Weltanschauung* began to disintegrate all along the line.

At last I returned to Russia to occupy the chair of political economy I had longed for. By that time I was in a state of complete spiritual resignation, through which the voice of religious faith sounded, at first timidly and uncertainly but then more and more victoriously. I began to profess this faith in my writings from 1901 and 1902 onwards, much to the surprise and indignation of my former comrades in thought. But basically, even as a Marxist in a state of spiritual barbarism, I always longed for religion and I was never indifferent to faith. Initially, I had a passionate emotional belief in an earthly paradise. Then, after a certain moment when I gave myself permission to do so, I took a sharp turn and went quickly and decidedly straight from the far country to my spiritual fatherland. Having regained faith in a 'personal' God, instead of the impersonal idol of progress, I accepted Christ—whom I had loved and carried in my heart as a child. And finally, I returned to Orthodoxy.

I was irresistibly drawn to my native Church. However, for years the thought of returning to my Father's house and the longing to do so remained unrealized. Secret suffering was the price I had to pay for my return. I was returning, of course, not only in heart but in mind as well. From a sociologist I was turning into a theologian (I note with gratitude the spiritual influence of Dostoyevsky and Vladimir Solovyov upon me in those years). At the same time there arose within me a desire, which secretly indeed had never left me, to return to my Father's house completely and become a priest. In those years I sometimes spoke of myself to my friends as a 'traitor to the altar'. It was not enough that I should have changed my philosophy of life. My Levite blood asserted itself more and more: my soul longed for priesthood and the altar. Prince E. N. Trubetskoy said to me once that he felt as though I 'had been born in a cassock'.

There were various obstacles in my way: to begin with, the habits and prejudices of my 'set' and even of my family. In the clerical environment in which I was raised it was an accepted and understood thing that at a certain time in life a man took Holy Orders. But among the intelligentsia atheism was the accepted thing, and to become a priest, at any rate for a Moscow University professor with a doctorate in political science to do so, was scandalous, eccentric, and certainly meant estranging oneself from enlightened society.[1] It required some resolution, and that took time. But I had made up my mind on the matter, and, besides, times were changing. I do not know, however, how I should have overcome all of my personal difficulties, but that the hand of God was obviously supporting me.

Early in 1918 news was received in Moscow that the Bolsheviks were shelling Yalta and the southern shore of the Crimea. My family lived there, and all communication with them was severed. There were reasons to fear that they had all perished. I remained alone before the face of God. Then I knew that nothing was holding me back and that there was no reason to delay the step that I had been contemplating in my heart for at least ten years. There had been another humanly insurmountable obstacle: the link between Orthodoxy and autocracy, which resulted in a pernicious and humiliating dependence of the Church upon the state and in a

[1] I have been told that Karl Kautsky, one of the leaders of German Social Democracy, exclaimed in surprise: '*Und Bulgakoff ist fromm geworden!*' (which is to say, 'So Bulgakov has gone batty!').

curious kind of caesaro-papism. This I could not get over, and it was not right that I should. Now in 1917 this obstacle was suddenly removed by the revolution. The Church proved to be free, and instead of being the State established, it became the persecuted Church. At the All-Russian Council (of which I was a member) the Church acquired a worthy and fearless leader in the person of Patriarch Tikhon. The Council was a canonical organ of the ecclesiastical government.

Together with the Church, I too gained freedom of action and had no time to lose before the approaching menace of the future. I made my decision and could no longer postpone it. At a late hour one evening, Prince E. N. Trubetskoy rang me up and gave me a friendly warning in Latin that I should be arrested that very night. As it happened, I developed pains and a fever when I retired that night. When the doctor arrived in the morning he diagnosed appendicitis, though he did not insist on an immediate operation. I had to disappear from my flat (though the warning from Trubetskoy proved to be a false alarm).

When I had somewhat recovered from my attack, I approached Bishop Feodor Volokolamsky, one of the Patriarch's vicars in Moscow, and asked if he would consent to ordain me priest. He knew me personally and had ordained my friend Professor Pavel Florensky. Upon his consent, I explained to him that my situation was urgent, for I was subject to arrest at any time. He had originally proposed that I should remain deacon for some time, but when he knew how matters stood he gave up that idea. Subsequently I applied to Patriarch Tikhon himself for permission to be ordained, and he graciously agreed without raising any objection. He laughed and said to me: 'You are more useful to us in a frock-coat than in a cassock.'

On 9 June 1918, the eve of the Feast of Pentecost, I set off for the Danilov Monastery carrying a bundle with clerical garb in it. On my return I carried a similar bundle containing the suit I had been wearing. I went to Bishop Feodor's and there I spent the night. (Those familiar with Moscow will know this monastery and its churchyard in which the mortal remains of Gogol, Khomyakov, and others lie resting.)

On Pentecost I was ordained deacon. If one could express the

BBA

inexpressible, I would compare this first ordination to a burning flame. The most striking moment occurred when I passed through the Royal Doors and approached the Holy Table for the first time. It was like going through fire, scorching, cleansing, and regenerating. It was entrance into another world, into the kingdom of heaven. It initiated for me a new state of being in which I have lived ever since. As I walked home through the streets of Bolshevik Moscow in a cassock, probably looking obviously unaccustomed to it, I did not hear a single rude remark, nor did I sense a single hostile glance. A little girl greeted me with a friendly 'Good morning, Father'. It was exactly the same the next day, when I came home as a priest. My cook, the wonderful Annushka, who had watched developments throughout with a silent sympathy, came up to me saying 'Bless me, Father' and was the first to receive my blessing (and after her, our hall porter).

On Whit Monday Bishop Feodor was to officiate at the cemetery church of the Holy Spirit, and we went there in procession from the Danilov monastery. Wearing an alb and carrying a deacon's candle, I walked beside the bishop. We had to walk some distance but met with no obstruction whatever.

Friends who happened to be in Moscow at the time came to the church for my ordination. I recall among them Father Pavel Florensky (with his son Vassia), who took part in the Liturgy, M. A. Novosyolov, N. N. Preiss, Vyacheslav Ivanov, N. A. Berdyaev, P. B. Struve, Prince E. N. Trubetskoy, G. A. Rachinsky, V. K. Horoshko, A. S. Glinka (Volzhsky), M. O. Gershenson, L. I. Shestov, S. A. Askoldov, and others. After the service there was a friendly tea party, hospitality arranged for us by the parish clergy (it was not an easy thing to do at that time).

The experience of this second ordination was even less describable than that of the first—I can only keep silent about it. Bishop Feodor addressed his sermon to me in the sanctuary, which moved me deeply, though now I cannot recall what he said. There was a general rejoicing and I felt a kind of serene triumph, a sense of eternity. The days of agony were over, like the sorrow of Holy Week melting in the light of Easter. What I experienced then was just that Easter joy.

My first liturgies were celebrated in the church of Our Lady 'the Joy of all the Sorrowful' at the orphanage on Zubov Boulevard where I lived. I officiated together with and under the guidance of Father Pavel Florensky, who spent a few days in Moscow after my ordination for the purpose. I was appointed to the church of St Elijah near the temple of St Saviour and celebrated several liturgies there before I left Moscow.

By then I had received news of my family and was to meet them in my new role. And so, a fortnight after my ordination, with the Patriarch's blessing I left for the Crimea to spend a month with them. After that I proposed to return to the place of my former work as a professor and of my new work as a priest. But I was not destined to return to Moscow at all.

On my way to the Crimea I had to pass near Kursk into the zone of German occupation. I was without a passport but got through successfully. I safely met my family and spent my month of leave with them. Then I tried to return to Moscow through Kiev, but circumstances had changed. After a month of vain attempts, I was forced to return to the Crimea. I remained there till the beginning of 1923, when I was exiled from Russia forever.

Glory be to God for everything!

My Conversion

How did I come to lose my faith? I lost it without noticing it myself. It occurred as something self-evident and unavoidable when the poetry of my childhood was squeezed out of my life by the prose of seminary education. As soon as I experienced my first doubts, and my critical faculty was early awakened, I realized that I could not be satisfied with the apologetics of the text-books. Instead of helping me, they further undermined my faith. My seminary education constantly raised before me many religious problems, but I was unable to cope with them, and the instructions given to me by my teachers only confused my mind. This conflict was further aggravated by compulsory attendance at the long services. Orthodox piety only irritated me, for its mystical side had ceased to exist for me.

I was twenty-four years old. For a decade I had lived without faith and, after early stormy doubts, a religious emptiness reigned in my soul. One evening we were driving across the southern steppes of Russia, and the strong-scented spring grass was gilded by the rays of a glorious sunset. Far in the distance I saw the blue outlines of the Caucasus. This was my first sight of the mountains. I looked with ecstatic delight at their rising slopes. I drank in the light and the air of the steppes. I listened to the revelation of nature. My soul was accustomed to the dull pain of seeing nature as a lifeless desert and of treating its surface beauty as a deceptive mask. Yet, contrary to my intellectual convictions, I could not be reconciled to nature without God.

Suddenly, in that evening hour, my soul was joyfully stirred. I started to wonder what would happen if the cosmos were not a desert and its beauty not a mask or deception—if nature were not death, but life. If he existed, the merciful and loving Father, if nature was the vesture of his love and glory, and if the pious feelings of my childhood, when I used to live in his presence, when I loved him and trembled because I was weak, were true, then the tears and inspiration of my adolescence, the sweetness of my prayers, my innocence and all those emotions which I had rejected and trodden down would be vindicated, and my present outlook with its emptiness and deadness would appear nothing more than blindness and lies, and what a transformation it would bring to me!

In 1898 a new wave of intoxication with this world came upon me. I experienced 'personal happiness'. I met the West for the first time. My admiration of its culture, its comfort, and its social democracy was boundless; and then suddenly a wonderful encounter with Raphael's Sistine Madonna took place in Dresden. It was a foggy autumn morning. I went to the art gallery in order to do my duty as a tourist. My knowledge of European painting was negligible. I did not know what to expect. The eyes of the Heavenly Queen, the Mother who holds in her arms the Eternal Infant, pierced my soul. I cried joyful and yet bitter tears, and with them the ice melted from my soul, and some of my psychological knots were loosened. This was an aesthetic emotion, but it was also a new knowledge; it was a miracle. I was then still a Marxist, but I was obliged to call my contemplation of the Madonna by the name of 'prayer'. I went to the Zwinger gallery early in the mornings in order to be there before others arrived. I ran there every day to pray and weep in front of the Virgin, and few experiences in my life were more blessed than those unexpected tears.

One sunny autumn day in 1908 I made my way to a solitary hermitage lost in the forest, where I was surrounded by the familiar sights of northern nature. I was still in the clutches of doubt and hesitation. I had come there as a companion of a friend; secretly I hoped that I might meet God. But my determination deserted me, and while I was at Vespers I remained cold and unfeeling. When the prayers for those preparing for confession began, I almost ran out of the church. I walked in deep distress towards the guest house, seeing nothing around me, and suddenly found myself in front of the elder's cell. I had been led there. I intended to go in another direction but absent-mindedly made a wrong turn in the confusion of my distress.

A miracle had happened to me. I realized it then without

any doubt. The Father, seeing his prodigal son, ran to meet me. I heard from the elder that all human sin was like a drop of water in comparison with the ocean of divine love. I left him, pardoned and reconciled, trembling and in tears, feeling myself returned as on wings within the precincts of the Church. At the door of the chapel I met my surprised and delighted companion, who had seen me leave in a state of acute distress. He was the witness of this conversion in my life.

It was another evening and another sunset, but this time a northern and not a southern one. The bells were calling to prayer. I listened to them as if I heard them for the first time in my life, for they invited me also to join the fellowship of believers. I looked on the world with new eyes. The next morning at the Eucharist I knew that I was a participant in the Covenant, that our Lord hung on the cross and shed his blood for me and because of me; that the most blessed meal was being prepared by the priest for me, and that the gospel narrative about the feast in the house of Simon the leper and about the woman who loved much was addressed personally to me. It was on that day when I partook of the blessed body and blood of my Lord.

Hagia Sophia

Yesterday for the first time in my life I had the happiness of seeing Hagia Sophia. God bestowed this favour upon me and has not let me die without a vision of St Sophia, and I thank my God for this. I experienced such heavenly bliss that it submerged—if only for a moment—all my present sorrows and troubles and made them insignificant. St Sophia was revealed to my mind as something absolute, self-evident, and irrefutable. Of all the wonderful churches I have seen, this is the most absolute, the universal church. The words of the Easter anthem ring in my mind: 'Lift up thine eyes, O Zion, and behold: thy children have come to thee from the west and the north and the sea and the east shining with the divine light.'

Human tongue cannot express the lightness, the clarity, the simplicity, the wonderful harmony which completely dispels all sense of heaviness—the heaviness of the cupola and the walls. A sea of light pours from above and dominates all this space, enclosed and yet free. The grace of the columns and the beauty of their marble lace, the royal dignity—not luxury, but regality—of the golden walls and the marvellous ornamentation: it captivates and melts the heart, subdues and convinces. It creates a sense of inner transparency; the weightiness and limitations of the small and suffering self disappear; the self is gone, the soul is healed of it, losing itself in these arches and merging into them. It becomes the world: I am in the world and the world is in me. And this sense of the weight on one's heart melting away, of liberation from the pull of gravity, of being like a bird in the blue of the sky, gives one not happiness nor even joy, but bliss. It is the bliss of some final knowledge of the all in all and of all in oneself, of infinite fullness in multiplicity, of the world in unity.

This is indeed Sophia, the real unity of the world in the Logos, the co-inherence of all with all, the world of divine ideas. It is Plato baptized by the Hellenic genius of Byzantium —it is his world, his lofty realm to which souls ascend for the contemplation of Ideas. The pagan Sophia of Plato beholds herself mirrored in the Christian Sophia, the divine Wisdom. Truly, the temple of St Sophia is the artistic, tangible proof and manifestation of St Sophia—of the Sophianic nature of the world and the cosmic nature of Sophia. It is neither heaven nor earth, but the vault of heaven above the earth. We perceive here neither God nor man, but divinity, the divine veil thrown over the world. How true was our ancestors' feeling in this temple, how right they were in saying that they did not know whether they were in heaven or on earth! Indeed they were neither in heaven nor on earth, they were in St Sophia—between the two: this is the *metaxu* of Plato's philosophical intuition. St Sophia is the last silent testimony to future ages of the Greek genius: a revelation in stone. Decadent Byzantines were unable to grasp it and express it in theological terms, and yet it lived in their hearts as the loftiest truth, conceived in Hellenism and made manifest in Christianity.

And it was no accident that it was here, in the temple of St Sophia, that the divine Sophianic symphony of Orthodox worship, inspired by her, took shape and sounded in the fullness of beauty. Here one understands anew the whole force and convincing self-evidence of the testimony of St Justin Martyr, the full meaning of which he himself did not know, that Socrates and Plato were Christians before Christ; for Plato was the prophet of Sophia in paganism.

The church of St Sophia is Plato's realm of ideas in stone rising above the chaos of non-being and subduing it through persuasion: the actual *pleroma*, all as a single whole, pan-unity. Here it is manifested and shown to the world. O Lord, how holy, how marvellous, how precious is this manifestation!

The Episcopate

Like the Church of Rome, Orthodoxy too, as it developed first in Byzantium and then in the Russian East of the Church of Moscow, suffers from papalism—not consciously dogmatic, clearly or responsibly formulated, but actual and psychological. Orthodoxy is grounded in *sobornost*, the communality of the body of the Church, and not in episcopacy, the bishop or bishops alone, and on this account it cannot be regarded as a parody, I should say a caricature, of Roman ecclesiastical autocracy and absolutism. Nevertheless there is a peculiar kind of exaggeration prevalent in the Russian and other Slavic churches with regard to episcopacy. (Fortunately, this disease seems to be much less virulent in the Greek Church, the birthplace of Orthodoxy, which indeed suffers from a certain ecclesiastical laxity offensive to our sense of piety.)

I have to make this confession hoping that as a voice from the grave it will carry more weight and not be vitiated by any personal considerations. In my lifetime I endure the evil in silence, and my silence is partly due to lack of courage and partly to the aversion I feel to the petty scandal to which such a protest of a little Russian Luther would inevitably give rise. As a matter of fact it has nothing to do with Lutheranism or a desire to undermine the gracious power of episcopacy, which is to me a mystical reality as evident as daylight. My 'Lutheranism' is a struggle not against but for episcopacy, a striving to reclaim it in its true dignity, to free it from the contamination of despotism, based on a slavish psychology.

This slavishness is to be found first of all in the attitude of the bishops to secular power, in caesaro-papism—the 'union of the church with the state', in substituting the kingdom of this world for the kingdom of God. (Such an attitude is found in Imperial Byzantium, Tsarist Russia, the Soviet Union, Polish nationalism, and various racialisms.) While thus submitting to Caesar outside the Church, the bishops have demanded the same submission to themselves within the

Church—not of course from the laity, who have remained free
and in a sense exercise power over the bishops, but from the
clerics bound by canonical obedience.

Such an abuse of the pastoral power and the tendency
towards despotic autocracy is psychologically made worse by
the fact that, contrary to the second canon of the Sophia
Council (which excluded monks from episcopal office), our
episcopate has been confined to monks—or rather, to pseudo-
monks since the vows of obedience became a step for obtaining
episcopal power and lost all relation to monastic spiritual
discipline.

Owing to the actual conditions of Russian Church life,
taking monastic vows for the sake of an episcopal career
became one of the most painful peculiarities of our ecclesiastical system; everybody knows this. The intolerable spiritual
contradiction involved in this has become more and more
manifest, especially in our time, when due to war and revolution secular authorities constantly supersede one another.
Each new regime has its own incumbents and power élite,
and the episcopacy is filled to an alarming extent by men bent
on making a career. All this must inevitably lead to a purifying
crisis in the life of the Church that will save it not from
episcopacy but, in its name, from bishops of a certain type.
St Seraphim is said to have prophesied that such a time would
come for the Russian Church.

No doubt the position of the episcopate is psychologically
difficult in itself: it harbours the danger of a peculiar kind of
man-worship. This has always been the case, both in the Old
Testament and beyond the confines of revealed religion. It
was not an accident that Christ's bitterest enemies and
persecutors were the high priests Annas and Caiaphas—the
whole ideological, confessional, and religious (man-deifying)
complex is involved in their rejection of Christ. And, alas,
this type of the Old Testament high priest has continued to
repeat itself in the history of the New Covenant. There is a
paradox here: high-priesthood is a divine institution in the
Old Testament, but historically and psychologically it is
dearly paid for by fallen humanity, frail in its sinfulness. It is
wrong defiantly to reject the divine institution itself on the
ground of human sinfulness, as Protestantism has done, but

it is also wrong to make an idol of it and worship it slavishly. This is a peculiar tragedy of Church life.

In the Roman Church it has found expression in the anthropotheism of the papacy and in the East in the papalist tendencies of the episcopate in the dogmatic and canonical sphere and in everyday life and customs. In the Russian Church one of the most important practical expressions of this tendency is the liturgical cult of episcopacy which imparts to divine worship the character of bishop-worship. The people love this ceremonial, they are brought up on it in the Church and, of course, are demoralized by this style of piety. The central nerve of prayerful life—the divine liturgy—is overshadowed by the pomp of episcopal ritual, by the decorative and therefore religiously pernicious lengthening of the service. The real acting of it is only felt within the sanctuary, for the ikon-screen to some extent protects the congregation from the provoking spectacle; but it is difficult to think and speak calmly of this introduction of decorative show into the holy of holies under the pretext of piety.

Enthusiasm for this pageantry is most frequently encountered among the less spiritual members of the episcopate, who assume the role of living ikons. But, alas, the temptation is real for all, and the most difficult aspect of the matter is that all of this tragic glorification of the episcopate is based not upon recognized dogma but upon ecclesiastical psychology and is a matter of feeling. Basically everything is undamaged and as it should be, but psychologically the Church is affected by the spiritual disease of man-worship.

In any case, I must confess that for all my affection and respect for the bishops with whom I personally had contact, this ecclesiastical despotism was the heaviest cross I had to bear as a priest, and I feel guilty of passivity, of connivance. Invariably when I read in church the Lord's severe words denouncing 'Moses' seat', my voice shook helplessly with secret pain. Such is the bitter truth of this aspect of my priesthood.

Another bitter truth concerns what I may call my liturgical destiny. I took Holy Orders solely in order to officiate, chiefly to celebrate the divine liturgy. In my naïve and inexperienced way I discerned very little as to the actual position of a priest in the Church. It soon became very apparent to me that in order to officiate one had to have a church, or in any case an altar. When I became a priest I was too old to follow the usual path of a priestly career from the beginning. In addition, my ordination came at a time of bitter Church persecution in Russia, and afterwards in exile I lived among refugees who had very few churches. As a result, during the quarter century of my priesthood I never had a church of 'my own' but always either con-celebrated with a bishop or vicar or occasionally took a service by myself, though never on great holy days. On such occasions as Holy Week and Easter my friends tried to arrange services for me in private houses, and this almost always meant a struggle in self-defence. To my knowledge, no bishop has ever sought to provide me with a church. My position in this respect was a heavy cross to bear as a priest and those near and dear to me shared my personal unhappiness. I cannot think of this calmly even now, when illness has made it impossible for me to officiate unaided. The psychological source of such indifference on the bishops' part is the same as I have indicated above.

There is much in the practice and customs of Orthodoxy that gives cause for sorrow—sacerdotalism, lack of culture and enlightenment in Church life, ritualism, superstition, and ignorant formalism—in fact everything that makes our Orthodoxy unorthodox; and yet it is all redeemed by the gracious gift of love for God. The fiery ordeal through which Russia is passing has brought to light both the Orthodox people's spiritual helplessness in their struggle with Bolshevik demonism directed against religious faith and holiness, and the special religious genius and vocation of the Russian people and their love of God. Such gifts could only be manifested in all their force and magnitude in the times of trial by which the Lord in his mercy has honoured the Russian people and their Church. I thank and glorify my God for having allowed me to enter the ranks of the clergy to serve him precisely in these terrible and tragic times when the Church's outer prosperity is at its lowest ebb.

All that has been said does not shake or limit my loyalty and devotion to Orthodoxy but merely frees it from all 'orthodoxism' natural to a *local* church unconscious of its narrow provincialism, which takes itself to be universal and all-embracing; breathing with one lung only, or with a part of it, it feels as though it were breathing fully. 'Ecumenism' as a fact means dissatisfaction with provincialism whether of the Roman or of the Eastern Byzantine type. One may in a kind of ecclesiastical conceit imagine oneself to embrace the whole fullness of the Church, but there is bound to remain a dim consciousness that this is not the case. That which was given and commanded to us has been lost in the distant past, but to this day it remains as a promise, a longing, an unsatisfied desire, as an open embrace that has nothing to clasp and cannot be replaced by brandishing a fist at the 'orthodox' who think differently. There should always be in one's heart a living pain at the Church's division and a sincere prayer 'for the union of all', given us as a promise and set us as a task in life. Till this is fulfilled, there can be no ecumenical Orthodoxy. I am speaking of the catholicity or universality of Orthodoxy —not of the dogmatic doctrine or the purity of tradition, but of the *feeling* of the Church. Hitherto this feeling of universality has not found adequate expression.

But I am even more conscious of another and perhaps more important divergence from 'historical' Orthodoxy. It has to do with the future, with eschatology, with the tremulous expectation and longing for the coming of Christ; Orthodoxy seems somehow to have lost this, not in its dogma but in fact, under the overwhelming burden of its historical heritage. The loss is even more evident in Roman Catholicism. Tradition has ceased to be 'vital' and has become the depository of the the faith, to be preserved but not developed creatively. Yet Orthodoxy demands not the mere possession of the inherited wealth of faith and life, but prophecy and apocalypse—a call and a promise. In this sense apocalypse implies a concern for the history of the present and the future as well as that of the past. The Church has no continuing city on earth, but seeks one to come. Orthodoxy implies inspiration, the *eros* of the Church, her yearning for the Bridegroom, the feeling proper to his Bride. It is creativeness directed towards the final goal, the expectation of the End. It is not cowardly fear of life and flight from it, but the overcoming of all givenness, the longing for a new heaven and a new earth, for a new meeting and life with Christ. All this is ineffable and sounds like music in the soul; it is like a symphony of colours, like art and poetry. It is eager expectation of the promise. 'Even so, come, Lord Jesus.'

Much as I am 'rooted' in the Church and at one with everything in it, in this feeling for her life I have remained solitary and alien to historical Orthodoxy, which has not satisfied me. Or, rather, I feel that to accept this limited sense of Orthodoxy is to betray it and to lose something vital and precious. It is almost impossible for me to put this feeling into words or to communicate it to others: it is like the reason of the heart; it brings together those lost in the sea of life and unites them in a bond of brotherhood as a Church within the Church.

I may refer to this experience as a Sophianic feeling for life which allows us to recognize the divine ground of the world under the crust of matter. I cannot say that I have been alone in this recognition—kindred spirits joined me and were near me—but so far as the institutional Church is concerned, I am lonely and cold in it. And yet so firm is my hope, so apocalyptic my attitude towards life, that I am supreme and joyous in my expectation. In the light of it I behold the present and foresee that which is to come; I seek the prophetic meaning of events and grasp their hidden significance, finding in them the fulfillment of the promised future.

In the light of the apocalypse I comprehend the historical tragedy which is being unfolded before us, and especially its main chapters or themes. Two of them glow for me with particularly vivid light: the destinies of Russia, my native land, and of Israel. All that is happening in the world seems to me to be centred in them, and they hold a special place in my thought; I am drawn to them more than to anything else in attempting to interpret prophecies. The terrible and as it were preordained destinies of these two peoples indicate their exceptional significance in the life of mankind as a whole. At the present time they are becoming more than ever before the centre of the world's history.

I do not expect to see the fulfillment of my prophetic hopes in my lifetime. So be it; it is God's will. But this does not undermine the firmness of my faith, the certainty of the expectation, any more than it drowns the victorious cry of the heart: 'Even so, come, Lord Jesus!' I am expecting a miracle in history—the revelation in it of its higher meaning, of the divine will. This can only happen through a manifestation of the fullness of biblical Christianity in the spirit and power of prayer and prophecy.

Dying before Death

I watched my first operation in a mirror in the ceiling just above me: all the details of the tracheotomy were reflected in it, and although I was in pain, I was interested. At the second operation they took care that I should not be able to see it, and, besides, my mind was dulled by narcotics. Nevertheless I heard what was being said and as far as possible observed what was happening. I was fully conscious, feeling of course all the pain, but not any fear. The divine power saved me from fear and dejection, and I recall this with profound and joyful gratitude. I was in a kind of ecstasy which I was able to communicate to other people too. On the Saturday and Sunday before the operation I confessed and gave communion to my friends, took leave of them, and so far as I could judge there was no sadness in them any more than in me. There was only the ecstasy of love. And I have always considered myself timid, and do so still, so that I regard that joy as a divine miracle, the action of the Holy Spirit. Of course I was anxious about my family, and my heart was heavy on their account, but even this was somehow miraculously kept in bounds. It was in this state of mind that I arrived at the clinic on the eve of the operation, calm and in good spirits.[1] The first operation was followed by a second

[1] This is what I wrote (to my own surprise, for I had long given up noting down anything for myself) not long before my operation: '6.III.1939. Thy Will be done. Today death looked me in the face—either from cancer of the vocal chords or from the operation which may be fatal, and in any case would make me dumb. I accept God's Will humbly and obediently, even calmly. I dare not say that I have "a desire to depart and to be with Christ", but I serenely look forward to the life beyond the grave. Only the fate of my dear ones and the thought of parting from them sends a pang to my heart, but I trust that the Lord Who rules over life and death will not forsake them. I am trying to think with whom and how I should be reconciled, whom I should comfort and be kind to, what I ought to do. . . . I am trying to remember everyone and forget nothing. May the Lord send His bright angel. Once I died spiritually in my ordination; now, dying bodily, I should like to be at peace and love everyone. . . . Glory be to God for everything!'

after a fortnight—on the Tuesday in Holy Week. I lost the power of speech after the first operation and instinctively began using the pencil instead. Somehow it seemed the natural thing to do and was not even particularly irksome.

My sufferings began in the Holy Week when the larynx had been removed. In the first place, it was agonizingly difficult to breathe, and the stifling, horrible, disgusting dressings made me into a kind of stiff bundle, so that I could neither move nor sleep. Of course I was deprived of food as well, for I could not open my mouth to swallow or pass any food down my throat, which had been cut open. A disgusting tube was stuck into my nose, through which some nasty liquid was poured in. ' "I thirst." And they gave him vinegar to drink' (John 19.28). The most agonizing part of it all was not pain but breathlessness, absence of air, together with mortal, unendurable weakness. I had several attacks of terrible, deadly breathlessness —chiefly at night—when in fact I was on the point of death. During the whole of my illness I had never experienced anything so agonizing as that. Sometimes the attacks were comparatively short but acute, and sometimes prolonged and accompanied by a confused, semi-delirious condition; and altogether I was never free from the humiliating dependence upon the contraption which cleared (or more often failed to clear) the mucus from my breathing. It was a state of dying —with intervals but without hope. I was plunged into a kind of darkness and lost the sense of space and time; I only vaguely remembered that it was Holy Week and that Good Friday and Lady Day were at hand. I was chronologically aware that Easter came, received Easter greetings, but the Gethsemane darkness was not dispelled and was unendurable; there was no Easter joy for the dying man to whom it was not given to taste death. No, there was no nearness of death, but mere dying.

In the past it had been given me to know death with its joy and liberation, but now I only felt its heavy fetters and darkness. What was there left of the joy and the ecstasy vouchsafed to me before the operation? Apparently nothing, or, rather, worse than nothing—only a shadow of death in the nethermost pit. The light of life was extinguished, and unhallowed insensibility came over me, of which it has been

said, 'Why hast Thou forsaken me?' True, there remained a
dull awareness that I was in the power of the Almighty and
that it was his will that devoted me to suffering or somehow
allowed it as inevitable. So far as I could remember, I did not
think of death for a moment. I was not expecting it or feeling
the horror of it—my mind was dulled and my thinking powers
much too feeble. In my dying I was too far from the light of
death—I was engrossed with my breathlessness, my soul was
devastated by physical suffering. There was no more prayer
as a way of ascending to God, just as there was no ascending
for the 'forsaken'. There was a joyless night without dawn,
without morning. There remained a sense of physical suffering,
but even this paled by comparison with the general sense of
having lost the power of spirit, of being forsaken; that,
perhaps, was the most terrible of all.

What, then, remained in me that was still human—if it
remained at all? Yes, something did remain, and that was as
it were the last miracle in my tortured soul—it was love. I
loved my fellow-men; I loved everyone. In my mind I lovingly
went over those whom I had known in the past, both the loved
and the unloved ones—those whom it was easy and joyous
and those whom it was difficult for me to love. I did nothing
but love—love all whom I remembered. I do not know
whether it was love in God. I believe it was; it probably was,
or else how could I love? Of course some of the people who
were at my bedside gave me more joy than others, some
comforted me by their presence and others wearied me, but
no one could disturb the harmony of love which somehow
broke through the discords of my deathlike days.

But where was my thought which had always burned in
me? Where were the 'problems' that had always worried me?
Where was the complex of exalted and inspiring ideas which
had not left me even when I came into this hospital? It all
seemed to have been extinguished, to have ceased to exist.
I was empty and evidently no longer capable of thought. My
existence was impoverished and became a simple bodily
existence, merely a capacity for suffering. Was I conscious
of God's nearness? Yes, in so far as nothing separated me from
God except bodily suffering, since everything else was gone.
This nearness to God, this standing face to face with him

made me tremble. At no time during my illness did I ever rebel against God in any way. I did not repine, did not ask him to spare me and deliver me from pain, accepting it as God's unchangeable and undoubted decree. And in this sense it was a holy and terrible nearness, like Job's. But it was not joyful; for it was throughout pervaded with one feeling: why hast thou forsaken me?

And yet, at the same time, there was something else that I had not known before and that was a true spiritual event for me. It will forever remain a revelation to me—not about death, but about dying with God and in God. That was my dying with Christ and in Christ. I was dying in Christ, and Christ was dying with me and in me. That was the terrible, the shattering revelation which perhaps I could not have expressed in words and concepts at the time but only recognized later. Only one incalculable single moment passed between 'Why hast Thou forsaken Me' and 'yielded up the ghost', between Christ's dying in his God-forsakenness and his death. But it contained timeless duration and completeness of dying for every man, in so far as he dies in and through it. A man cannot die except in a state of God-forsakenness, just as the universal man, the new Adam, could not die in his God-manhood. I knew Christ in my dying, I felt his nearness to me, an almost bodily nearness, but as of 'a bruised and mutilated corpse' lying beside me. He could only help me in my suffering and dying by suffering and dying with me. I saw that image with my inner vision and felt him as Holbein, and Dostoyevsky after him, felt him in the terrible picture of Christ's death. That painting, however, depicts not death but dying, not the power of transfiguration after death, coming with the resurrection and on the way to it, but a stationary death which does not go beyond dying. This was perfectly in keeping with the deathlike days of Holy Week which entered into and penetrated my whole being. In the past, when I was well, I rejected Holbein's corpse-like image as blasphemous and devoid of faith. Now it relived for me precisely as a presentation of death as dying, as a revelation about death through the human dying of the God-man.

There is another heart-rending image of Christ's suffering—Grünewald's Christ. But that was different and therefore did

not come into my mind: Grünewald's 'Crucifixion' is only an
element in the dialectic of death, indissolubly connected with
the resurrection in glory—which is expressed by other parts
of the polyptych. Grünewald gives a terrible image of death
as seen in the corpse after the dying has already taken place
and thus exhausted itself. But the image of the corpse in
Holbein's picture suggests the actual dying which is still
taking place, the very essence of it. That was how I felt it—
not by reason but by inner knowledge, when I lay together
with him, not dead but dying, not yet a corpse but corpse-
like, and not living though not dead. I could not—or was as
yet unable—to pray to this Christ but could only love him
and share in his suffering just as he shared in mine. Through
my human dying there was revealed to me his human dying
in his God-manhood; his divinity was, as it were, fading out
in God-forsakenness, and his humanity was dying. The dying
which took place in the God-man could only have taken place
humanly, i.e. in man's God-forsakenness. It identified itself
with all human dying and in that sense was universal, including within itself every aspect of death, every mortal illness,
and was the synthesis of them all. And the general content of
all these multifarious forms of dying was death. The God-man
in his God-forsakenness laid himself open and made himself
accessible to dying. Death approached him in his humanity.
And his dying was the agony of all human agonies. In its
humanity it was natural, i.e. it was not lightened by being
merged with the divine power.

In the final *kenosis* there took place as it were a division
between the two natures, not of course in the ontological
sense, since in Christ they are indivisible, but in the sense that,
while one was in abeyance, the other remained in its full force.
It is in this self-humiliation of the God-man that there lies
the saving power of his death; its human character leads to its
being divinely-human. Christ died our human death in order
to taste through it his death as the God-man. This is why our
dying, as dying with Christ, is a revelation about Christ's
death, though not as yet about his glory. Then I understood
the meaning of St Paul's words: 'Always bearing about in the
body the dying of the Lord Jesus, that the life also of Jesus
might be made manifest in our mortal flesh. So then death

worketh in us, but life in you' (2 Cor. 4.10–12). And also, 'The whole creation groaneth and travaileth in pain together until now. And not only they, but ourselves also, which have the first fruits of the Spirit, even we ourselves groan within ourselves, waiting for the adoption, to wit, the redemption of our body' (Rom. 8.22–3).

·

2

From Marxism to Idealism:
1903

Three essays from *Ot Markzisma k Idealizmou* (Moscow, 1903) indicating something of Bulgakov's journey from Marxism to Christianity and of the influence he felt from V. S. Solovyov and Fyodor Dostoyevsky.

Economic Ideals

Political economy is a practical discipline. It came into being owing to the practical importance which attaches at the present day to economic problems in the life of civilized nations. It was the fruit of the modern mind's quest for righteousness in economic life. It arose in answer to moral and not to intellectual demands. According to this preliminary definition, political economy is *applied ethics*, that is, the ethics of the economic life.

Consequently, political economy is not autonomous but heteronomous, and dependent upon the ideal which is set before it as a kind of axiom. But while we have not yet entered the domain of political economy and merely stand at the threshold of it, it is our right and duty critically to examine its final ideals which, as in every other technical discipline, are only relatively absolute. We can submit them to a critical test by connecting them with that which appears to us as truly absolute and unquestionable. We shall thus obtain certain guiding principles for deciding to what extent modern political economy fulfils its task and has a true and clear conception of it. We will consider from this point of view both the fundamental problems and the general subject-matter of present day political economy.

Two great problems are vital for it: the problem of the production of wealth and that of its distribution—the economic and the social questions. Hence the task of political economy is determined by two ideals: one economic and the other social. Inquiry into these two ideals, these two 'oughts' that are absolute for political economy, provides a critical introduction to it. In the present context we shall discuss only the first kind of 'ought' or, in other words, the ideal of economic policy.[1]

Freedom may be positive or negative. One may be free from material needs through not having them at all or through

[1] S. Bulgakov, *From Marxism to Idealism* (Moscow, 1903), pp. 264 ff.

having satisfied them. Thus a savage is free from the need for clothes because he goes about naked, and a civilized man is free from it because he has clothes. In a similar way, a baby and a saint are equally free from sin or vice, but the baby is free from it because its mind is so undeveloped that it cannot sin and is in a certain sense below sin. The saint is free from it because he has overcome sin and consequently is above it. In defining negative freedom one may go still further and maintain, for instance, that the dead are even more free than the savages, for they have no needs whatever. Obviously it is not this freedom of emptiness which is meant when people speak of the human spirit growing in freedom. Freedom is understood as positive power, as increasing possession of wealth and consequently as the increasing possibility for the human spirit to manifest and assert itself. In this sense wealth may be defined as the necessary condition of mankind's historical development, although taken by itself it does not make history. Poor and savage peoples dominated by the forces of nature have no history and stand outside it; liberation from primitive poverty is the beginning of history. Higher demands can only develop when the lower have been satisfied. It is not accidental that throughout history the highest development of a people's culture coincides with their greatest material prosperity; and vice versa, cultural decadence is accompanied by economic decline.

Once it has been recognized that growth of national wealth is a good thing, the conditions necessary to it must be accepted also. One of those conditions is the increase in needs which is, as it were, the reverse side of the increase in national wealth. In order to make this or that conquest of nature we must first feel the need for it. We must want to communicate with people in order to make use of the telephone or the post; we must want knowledge of the starry sky in order to use the telescope; we must want spiritual freedom and power in order to strive for mastery over nature. Increase in needs is a law not of material existence only, but of the spirit as well; spiritual development consists precisely in the fact that the spirit makes greater demands and discovers hitherto unsuspected tasks and problems.

We have thus arrived at the economic ideal and the basic

commandment of political economy: increase wealth and multiply your needs. The question has been settled positively, and the claims of political economy and its postulates have been recognized. We have seen, however, that this relatively absolute ideal is not in itself absolute or independent, as political economy takes it to be, but receives its sanction from something else, glows with a reflected light, and is admitted only as a means to an end. Hence it is not autonomous but heteronomous, and on all decisive issues of economic policy appeal must be made to a higher non-economic authority, for political economy is not self-sufficient. This, of course, does not prevent its ideal from being quite sufficient and within certain limits autonomous for the purposes of ordinary everyday economic life.[1]

Although as a philosophy of life asceticism must be rejected, the ascetic principle in morality is indisputable. Since the meaning of life is to be found not in pleasure but in spiritual goods, the inner life of man and of human society is a constant struggle between spirit and sensuality for domination. Economic progress lessens man's dependence upon nature as an external limitation but does not liberate him from his inner dependence upon his body. Wealth becomes a spiritual power, affecting man's spirit from within, and is thus transformed into a temptation. The dictum that one cannot serve both God and mammon retains its significance forever. Either the ideal or the lower, carnal principle in man gains the upper hand, and the lower ought always to be under the control of the spirit.

The right correlation between the different needs of the flesh and the spirit is achieved by means of spiritual struggle, described by the Greek word *askesis* (which really means exercise) or asceticism. Of course, forms and degrees of asceticism vary throughout history. The epoch when the spiritual principle of life was preached to savage barbarians required heroes of physical asceticism unthinkable in our day, when physical needs and general development are on quite a different level. But our epoch also knows of ascetics whose life is a constant spiritual struggle, perpetual sacrifice, and self-abnegation, although at present those ascetics are more

[1] Ibid., pp. 278 ff.

frequently met in secular life and not in the monastery or the desert. The beauty of ascetic or moral achievement is as attainable in our epoch as it was in the age of monastic asceticism. Surely a healthy moral sense is captivated by the image of Francis of Assisi, the apostle of voluntary poverty, even now; it is not likely to prefer the dissolute Cleopatra or the *roi-soleil*, who have a curious aesthetic attraction for a depraved taste. Of course the power of the spirit over sensuality, of God over mammon, is an inner moral act not necessarily connected with one set of external expressions. The latter are determined both by the individual's character and by the epoch. Hence the ascetic principle of morality does not as such conflict with the basic economic commandment of multiplying man's needs in so far as this leads to the liberation of historical mankind from the power of nature for the sake of creating a wider basis for spiritual culture. An asceticism that called us to renounce such achievements of civilization as railways, the post, the printing press, science, and literature would be reactionary obscurantism, defending not freedom of the spirit but its enslavement. On the other hand, the spiritual development of personality and a greater sense of human dignity inevitably find expression in, among other things, the increase of material needs; the modern democratic movement is an instance of this.

Here as everywhere else in moral life the decisive factor is man's spiritual nature, the direction of his will. Multiply your needs so long as this is required by human dignity and the life of the spirit, but also learn to curtail them when the spiritual life requires it—such is the formula free from the extremes both of hedonism and of asceticism. From this point of view it is possible to give a definition of luxury, which Zombart refuses to give, justly pointing out that it has no external distinguishing marks, and that the conception of it is changeable and relative. There are no outward characteristics of luxury, hence it can only be characterized inwardly, although with reference to a particular epoch it is not difficult to indicate its external manifestations. Luxury means the victory of sensuality over the spirit, of mammon over God in the individual soul or in a society as a whole; once the cult of pleasure, aesthetic or otherwise, becomes the guiding principle, we have to do with luxury. Luxury is the reverse side of wealth and its constant danger. In extreme poverty the freedom of the spirit is lost owing to external limitations and in wealth through succumbing to inner temptation. Luxury and destitution are equally anti-cultural, and equal spiritual poverty may reign in a beggar's hovel and in a grandee's palace.

The spiritual decadence involved in luxury sooner or later leads to material decadence as well, so that economically, too, luxury is self-condemned. A people's spiritual condition is by no means important for its economic life. No one would maintain that intemperance is better than temperance, or that moderation is worse than excess; and yet in picturing the future, the element of inner struggle between God and mammon in the human soul is completely overlooked. The modern mind, in over-mechanizing life, is particularly prone to imagine an ideal social system in which men will be virtuous as it were automatically, without any inner conflict. No, virtue is always won and built up only through moral struggle, and if it be our lot to struggle chiefly against destitution and all kinds of tyranny, future generations will have to struggle against, among other things, wealth and luxury. Wealth merely builds up the walls of civilization, but within these walls it may enclose either a bright temple or a house of ill fame.

This, I think, is the attitude to wealth which the gospel teaches us to adopt. It does not ban human joy or condemn all sensuous pleasures. But it warns us against ensnaring the spirit in cares about wealth and the morrow; it condemns those who put their trust in riches and commands us to make a decisive choice between serving God or mammon, since the two are incompatible. In addressing itself to the spiritual man and preaching life in spirit and in truth, the gospel avoids both abstract asceticism and, even more, sensuous hedonism, but it does not condemn culture and the economic progress necessary for it. Humanity must not bury its talent in the ground, as asceticism teaches it to do, but must increase it throughout history.[1]

---

[1] Ibid., pp. 281 ff.

Ivan Karamazov
as a Philosophical Type

Sitting in a wretched tavern Ivan Karamazov says to his brother Alyosha:

'. . . what have Russian boys been doing till now, some of them, I mean? In this stinking tavern, for instance, here, they meet and sit down in a corner. They've never met in their lives before and when they go out of the tavern, they won't meet again for forty years. And what do they talk about in that momentary halt in the tavern? Of the eternal questions, of course; of the existence of God and immortality. And those who do not believe in God talk of socialism or anarchism, of the transformation of all humanity on a new pattern, so that it all comes to the same, they're the same questions turned inside out. And masses, masses of the most original Russian boys do nothing but talk of the eternal questions. . . . Isn't it so?'

'Yes, for real Russians the questions of God's existence and of immortality, or, as you say, the same questions turned inside out, come first and foremost, of course, and so they should.'[1]

So says Alyosha in answer to him.

Ivan Karamazov is one of the central figures in this great epic which reflects the loftiest as well as the vilest aspects of Russian life. He is one of the three brothers Karamazov who perhaps symbolized for Dostoyevsky the whole of Russian society, indeed the whole of Russian life. At the same time Ivan is an episodic character in the novel and plays no active part in the plot. Ivan's relation to the tragedy that took place in the Karamazov's house can, at the worst, be described as connivance. Later on Ivan is tortured by the thought that he is morally responsible for the murder, but this is morbid delirium, indicative of his mental condition rather than of

[1] Dostoyevsky, Fyodor M., *The Brothers Karamazov*, tr. Constance Garnett (New York, 1950), pp. 277 f.

any part he may have taken. 'It was not you who murdered him',[1] Alyosha says to him, and Alyosha generally is the author's mouthpiece. And indeed it is not difficult to see that the catastrophe is coming with fatal inevitability, that the tragedy is unavoidable and would take place without Ivan's having any part in it. Objectively speaking, one might say that Alyosha, no less than Ivan, allowed it to happen.

Ivan's tragedy is not that he arrives at conclusions which deny morality; there are plenty of people for whom the theory that 'all things are lawful' serves merely as a convenient excuse for practical immorality; his tragedy is that his heart —'a lofty heart, capable of much suffering',[2] as the Elder characterizes it—cannot be reconciled with these conclusions. It is sufficient to recall how Ivan suffers from the thought that he is guilty of his father's murder. Theoretical reason is here in conflict with practical reason: that which logic denies speaks in the heart; in spite of all denials it exists as a fact of direct moral consciousness, as the voice of conscience. A highly moral nature is compelled to deny morality; such is the essence of this terrible conflict. It is like a person's having to deny the existence of daylight which he sees with his own eyes —with the difference that conflict with regard to a particular fact of knowledge cannot be compared in importance to a question that concerns a man's moral life as a whole.

Atheistic amoralism, as Ivan's ethical convictions may be called, is curiously reminiscent of the strivings of Friedrich Nietzsche. Everyone who has even a superficial acquaintance with Nietzsche's moral philosophy will easily see that his fundamental ideas and tendencies are identical with Ivan's. This is quite understandable, since they are both concerned with the same basic problem as to whether absolute morality is compatible with positivism. (I am leaving out, of course, the details of Nietzsche's philosophy, for by comparison with the ethical problem all else is of secondary importance.) The general idea that the superman and Ivan's man-god are beyond good and evil and that 'everything is lawful for them' is characteristic of both Nietzsche and Ivan; the rejection of altruism and the principle of egoism which takes the place of the old discarded morality are also common to both. The

---

[1] Ibid., p. 794. [2] Ibid., p. 80.

superman's egoistic grandeur, one morality for masters and
another for slaves, are the inevitable 'fruits of the heart's
emptiness' which is left when the morality of love and duty
is rejected. The spiritual drama of Friedrich Nietzsche and
Ivan Karamazov is one and the same—theoretical amoralism
incompatible with the moral demands of the heart. To my
mind, the greatness of Nietzsche's spirit finds expression
precisely in the passionate sincerity with which he faced this
conflict—a conflict that ended in the tragedy of his madness.
There is not and there cannot be any other way out of
Nietzsche's philosophy. If, having written all that he did write,
he had remained a comfortable philistine—for instance like
Voltaire after writing *Candide*, a book of despairing unbelief—
Nietzsche would simply have been a man of letters, treating
various philosophical subjects in highly finished prose or
verse. It is by his madness rather than by his writings that he
has shown the real importance and significance of the problems
of which he wrote. Nietzsche's life is a necessary commentary
on his writings, throwing a tragic light upon them and making
us understand his Zarathustra's real sufferings.

With the insight of genius Dostoyevsky formulated
Nietzsche's problem—the problem of atheistic amoralism;
but unlike Nietzsche, who wholly spent himself upon it,
Dostoyevksy, while understanding the problem, rose above
it; his spirit was broad enough to include Nietzsche-Ivan,
and Alyosha, and the prophetic spirit of Father Zossima. To
Dostoyevsky himself one might apply the words of the devil
about great ascetics whom he had tried to tempt: 'One soul is
worth a whole constellation.' 'They can contemplate such
depths of belief and disbelief at the same moment that sometimes it really seems that they are within a hair's breadth of
being "turned upside down".'[1]

[1] Cf. an extract from Dostoyevsky's notebook: 'The Inquisitor and
the chapter about children. In view of these chapters even a scholar like
you [apparently this refers to Kavelin] might treat me and my philosophy less haughtily—although philosophy is not my speciality. The
atheistic position has *never* been stated in Europe with such force. And
so it isn't as a child that I believe in Christ and profess Him; my
"hosannah" has passed *through a great crucible of doubt.*' In a letter
written in 1870 Dostoyevsky says, 'the question which has tortured
me consciously and unconsciously all my life is the existence of God.'

It is easy to see that the problems raised by Ivan are organically interconnected. They concern the most essential aspects of the nineteenth-century conception of the world. The chief inspiration of that century was faith in mankind's infinite progress; however much the various theories of progress may differ, they all imply this faith. Progress is an end in itself; there is no external imperative of any kind to justify it or make it into a means to some further and higher purpose. The meaning of progress is the greatest happiness of the greatest possible number. The basic rule of nineteenth-century morality is altruistic service of progress. The most striking and determined expression of this view is the theory of so-called scientific socialism, or of socialism in general. Theoretically speaking, socialism is only a particular form of the doctrine of progress as such; there may be other ways of conceiving mankind's further development, but historically it is the most important and in our day perhaps the only prevalent theory of progress. In this sense the theories of progress and socialism may be regarded as equivalent. Hence, all Ivan's doubts about the theory of progress also apply to socialism, considered not merely as an economic theory but as a general view of the world, indeed as a religion. Ivan expresses doubt about the three basic dogmas of that religion: about the binding character of moral norms commanding us to sacrifice to this impersonal progress or to other people's good our personal good and interests; about the *cost* of progress, as one might call it, in which the happiness of future generations is bought at the price of the unhappiness of the present (a purely eudaemonistic theory of progress); and finally about the future humanity for the sake of which all these sacrifices are made.

From what has been said you see that the pulse of the world's thought is beating in the little town where the Karamazovs live. Ivan Karamazov is a *universal* figure (though as yet very imperfectly understood and appreciated). In this novel Dostoyevsky shows himself to be the universal man whom he described with such impassioned eloquence in his speech on Pushkin.

Why is a sick conscience so characteristic of us Russians? The answer to this question is clear to everyone. It is because there is a tremendous gap, a terrible disharmony between our life and the demands of conscience and reason—and it is this disharmony that makes us ill. An ideal by its very nature does not correspond to reality and is a challenge to it, but the degree of discrepancy may vary. In Russia it is measured by centuries, for while the ideals of the educated class have kept pace with the most advanced European thought, our reality in many respects lags several centuries behind. This is why nowhere in Europe does life so offend, hurt, and maim people as it does in Russia. The moral pain of this discrepancy expresses itself in the minds of the intelligentsia as a feeling of moral responsibility towards the common people, a complete and fruitful union with whom is prevented by blind and as yet unconquered forces. Dostoyevsky expressed this heart-ache of the intelligentsia with the overwhelming simplicity of genius in one picture in that same novel. Mitya Karamazov, worn out by the investigating magistrate's questions, lies down on a large chest, falls asleep, and has a dream.

He was driving somewhere in the steppes where he had been stationed long ago, and a peasant was driving him in a cart with a pair of horses through snow and sleet. He was cold, it was early in November, and the snow was falling in big wet flakes, melting as soon as it touched the earth. And the peasant drove him smartly; he had a fair long beard. He was not an old man, somewhere about fifty, and he had on a grey peasant's smock. Not far off was a village. He could see the black huts and half the huts were burnt down; there were only the charred beams sticking up. And as they drove in, there were peasant women drawn up along the road; a lot of women, a whole row, all thin and wan, with their faces a sort of brownish colour, especially one at the edge, a tall, bony woman, who looked forty but might have been only twenty, with a long, thin face. And in her arms was a little baby crying. And her breasts seemed so dried up that there was not a drop of milk in them. And the child cried and cried, and held out its little bare arms, with its little fists blue from cold.

'Why are they crying? Why are they crying?' Mitya asked, as they dashed gaily by.

'It's the babe,' answered the driver, 'the babe is weeping.' And Mitya was struck by his saying in his peasant way 'the babe', and he liked the peasant's calling it a 'babe'. There seemed more pity in it.

'But why is it weeping?' Mitya persisted stupidly, 'Why are its little arms bare? Why don't they wrap it up?'

'The babe's cold, its little clothes are frozen and don't warm it.'

'But why is it? Why?' foolish Mitya still persisted.

'Why, they're poor people, burnt out. They've no bread. They're begging, because they've been burnt out.'

'No, no,' Mitya still did not understand. 'Tell me why is it those poor mothers stand there? Why are people poor? Why is the babe poor? Why is the steppe barren? Why don't they hug each other and kiss? Why don't they sing songs of joy? Why are they so dark from black misery? Why don't they feed the babe?'[1]

Throughout the nineteenth century the Russian intelligentsia has been constantly dreaming this dream. Now, in 1901, it is dreaming too that in many provinces stretching many thousands of miles, among many millions of population, 'the babe' is hungry and crying. Its crying reaches us but faintly, and we cannot even help it by our own efforts. Let this dream then continue to haunt us, and let our conscience remain uneasy so long as we have not the power to teach 'the babe' and to feed it, as long as it is 'poor and dark from black misery', as long as they 'don't hug each other and kiss and don't sing songs of joy!'

---

[1] Dostoyevsky, op. cit., p. 615f.

Vladimir Solovyov:
Scholar and Seer

What can Vladimir Solovyov's philosophy give to the modern mind? This question can only be answered if we first make clear what it is that men of the present day need most and are spiritually thirsting after. They long first and foremost for that which is the basic principle of Solovyov's philosophy, its alpha and omega—*the positive unity of all*. The consciousness of modern man is broken up; it has become a fragment of itself in and through the division of labour, but it never ceased to suffer from this fragmentation and to seek an integral world-conception which would connect the depths of reality with our everyday work; would give meaning to our personal life and set it *sub specie aeternitatis*. Solovyov's ideal of integral knowledge, integral life, and creativeness is natural to every cultured mind. And yet, in spite of all its wealth of knowledge and the high development of science, modern thought suffers from inner disruption and impotence. Elements which normally should be in harmony are either mutually hostile or disconnected; science suspects metaphysics of usurping its domain, and both metaphysics and science have the same suspicion with regard to religion. Meanwhile practical life goes its own way, independently of either.

This state of things cannot be regarded as either final or normal, but a way out of it can only be provided by an integrating philosophy which would reconcile for the modern mind religion, metaphysics, and science, throwing their united light on practical life with its moral and historical problems and on the domain of what 'ought to be'. Solovyov's philosophy is an essay in such synthesis, unique of its kind in modern times.

What has Solovyov's theory of knowledge to say to us? Generally speaking, all that epistemology can do is to settle the formal question as to the *validity* of this or that source of knowledge, of this or that doctrine. In this sense it may be said that Solovyov's theory widens and confirms the most precious and essential rights of the human mind. It critically justifies the ground of abstract thought, empirical knowledge, and faith; it shows that these are different ways of apprehending one and the same absolute first principle and that their normal inter-relation is unity and not hostility. There is thus established between them not a temporary compromise but inner peace and harmony. It is even more important that Solovyov's theory recognizes the validity of empirical, living, or 'concrete' knowledge; such knowledge indissolubly combines all the three sources of cognition: faith, reason, and experience. In the history of philosophy each one of these in turn has been put forward while the remaining two were rejected as folly, although living consciousness never renounced them and indeed never can. When theology and abstract clericalism were predominant, the rights of blind faith alone were recognized—faith unenlightened, as Solovyov put it, by 'profligate' reason and scientific knowledge. The flames of the Inquisition, which was ready to condemn to the stake all free inquiry, were lit to the glory of faith. Centuries passed, and faith suffered the same persecution from reason and science as it had once directed against them; the most sacred and legitimate demands of faith were ridiculed or simply ignored.

Meanwhile science and philosophical reason, temporarily united against their alleged common enemy, faith, began to quarrel and finally repudiated each other (Hegelianism and positivism). All this has brought philosophy to a crisis, and Solovyov indicates a way out of it. The results of philosophical development plainly show, says Solovyov, that it is utterly erroneous to oppose one to another the sources of knowledge taken in the abstract; harmony between them is both legitimate and necessary. He proclaims the inalienable rights of that living human consciousness which has been made a subject of philosophical vivisection; the recognition of these rights is here made by no primitive, naïve, unphilosophic mind, but as a logical inference drawn from a review of the whole agelong development of philosophy. The living human soul was not to be finally dried up in a monastery or dissected under a microscope or evaporated into an abstraction; like a phoenix it has risen anew from the ashes of history.

The real or positive unity of all reveals itself to the knowing spirit as truth; but

> the theoretical or cognitive element could only be separated from the moral or practical, and from the artistic or aesthetic, if the human spirit could be split up into several independent entities, one of which would be will only, another reason only, the third feeling only . . . In truth, however, the theoretical sphere of thought and knowledge, the practical sphere of will and activity, and the aesthetic sphere of feeling and artistic creativeness differ not in their component elements, which are the same in each, but only in the comparative predominance of one or another element in this or that sphere . . . If, then, truth, which is the content of true philosophy, must necessarily be related to will and feeling through satisfying their loftiest demands, the starting point of this truth—absolute reality—cannot be determined by the activity of thought alone but by will and feeling as well. And indeed absolute reality is demanded not only by our reason as the logically necessary presupposition of every particular truth, but also by the will as the necessary presupposition of all moral activity, as the absolute end or the good; and finally it is demanded by feeling as the necessary presupposition of perfect bliss, as eternal and absolute beauty which alone can overcome the apparent disharmony between sensuous phenomena and in one triumphal chord unite the painful jar of their discordant voices.[1]

The absolute first principle, the positive unity of all, is revealed to man under three aspects as truth, goodness, and beauty.

The existence of this divine or absolute principle is affirmed by faith alone. Solovyov is against all attempts to give a rational proof of the existence of God. 'The *content* of the divine principle, just like the content of external nature (the existence of which is also affirmed only by faith) is given in

[1] Solovyov, V. S., *Sobranie Sochinenii* (St Petersburg, 1911–14), I, pp. 316 ff.

experience. We believe that God *is*, and we learn by experience what He is.'[1] Religious experience and religious thought taken together constitute the content of religious consciousness. Since human spirit in general and therefore religious consciousness also is not a complete and ready-made entity, but comes into being, evolves, and grows in perfection, the revelation of the divine principle in that consciousness must inevitably also be gradual. Just as external nature only gradually reveals itself to the mind of man, and we have to speak of the development of experience and of science, so the divine principle too reveals itself to the human mind by degrees, and we must speak of the development of religious thought and experience. Since the divine principle is the actual object of religious consciousness, i.e., since it acts upon that consciousness and reveals itself to it, religious development is an objective and positive process, a real interaction between God and man—a divine-human process.

As we ascend the scale of ideas we reach at last an idea which is the unity of all others and contains everything. Such an idea must be defined as absolute love or the good. Every idea is love or the good for its bearer, every entity is that which it loves; the universal idea is absolute love or absolute good. Thus the fullness of ideas or the fullness of being must be conceived not as a mechanical totality but as their inner union which is love. We thus discover the basic conception of Solovyov's philosophy as a whole, its unchangeable centre. In the words of his poem that centre is 'the sun of love which only is at rest'.[2] Solovyov's ontology brings us to the formula 'God is love'.

Solovyov has the merit of developing the philosophical and theological idea of divine tri-unity on the basis of critical philosophy, and of formulating it in a way which satisfies the demands of modern speculative thought and disposes of the main philosophical difficulties of unitarian theism.

This philosophical theory brings us into the domain of positive Christian theology. As a doctrine, Christianity synthetically combines all the elements in the development

---

[1] Ibid., III, p. 31.
[2] Solovyov, V. S., 'Vnov Byelie Kolokolchniki', *Stichotvoreniya i Shutochniye Peci* (Munich, 1968), p. 188. [Ed.]

of religious consciousness noted above and also of the philosophical conception of God: the ascetic principle of Buddhism expressed in the view that 'the whole world lieth in wickedness'; Platonic idealism—the recognition of an ideal cosmos, 'heaven' beside 'earth'; the strict monotheism of the Jewish religion out of which Christianity arose; and finally, the Trinitarian doctrine organically following from the doctrine of the person of Christ.

The modern critical theology of Protestantism sterilizes Christianity, striving to banish from it the doctrine of the divinity of Christ and to reduce it to an ethic (to 'Kantianize' it). As against this, Solovyov rightly points out that the most essential content of Christianity is the doctrine of Christ as the God-man; the main features of Christian morality, on the other hand, are found also in pre-Christian religions (for instance, the doctrine of love in Buddhism—much as it differs from the Christian). Hence those who completely reject the unique significance of Christianity are more logical than those who are half-hearted about it.

It is not my purpose, however, to discuss the theological approach to the problem. In Solovyov's philosophy Christ is the unifying principle of the universal organism, of the real 'all'. Accordingly, we may distinguish in that organism the *formative* unity—the divine Logos or Christ—and the *formed* unity, receptive of the unifying activity of the Logos. Similarly, 'in every organism there are two kinds of unity: the unity of the active principle which reduces to itself as one the plurality of the elements, and on the other hand the plurality as reduced to unity, as the express image of that principle.' Solovyov calls this derivative unity by the biblical name of *Sophia*.

All his life Solovyov had to fight on two fronts: he denounced, on the one hand, those who have the name of Christ on their lips but crucify him in their lives and, on the other, those who serve Christ by their deed but reject him in their thought. This basic paradox of Russian life can be wholly removed only by great historical events which will radically change the conditions of the people's religious and political life; but until then it must be recognized for what it is. In Solovyov we find the clearest recognition of it, which is at the same time a prophetic anticipation of the future. He said that Christianity if it really is the universal truth must be realized in the collective life of mankind and be the supreme criterion for the valuation of all the facts and requirements of the day. In short, politics must be Christian. The chief sin of Byzantium, as Solovyov more than once pointed out, was that it only knew Christianity in the home and in the church, abandoning the whole sphere of social and political life to the base, irrational elements of human nature. Something similar is to be found in our modern life, and it is the duty of every sincere Christian to strive against this abnormal state of things.

One of the main achievements of Solovyov as a publicist is the right formulation and solution of the national question; his struggle against the later Slavophiles is well known and apparently no one disputes its value. It is therefore all the more interesting and more important to state Solovyov's views on the subject as a whole. In his polemics he had to argue against the extremes of nationalism and thus turn his back upon the idea of nationality as such. Hence people might imagine that Solovyov was a cosmopolitan, or, what comes to the same thing in practice, a 'westerner'. But this was not the whole case at all. Solovyov was a champion of universalism —not of a negative, cosmopolitan, non-national sort, but of a positive or super-national universalism. He often repeated that although Christianity is super-national, it does not reject nationality.

Unfortunately Solovyov never completely freed himself from Slavophile limitations and romanticism; his political ideas are far from clear. He simply restates the Slavophile theory with all its merits and defects, adding to it his own erroneous and unsatisfactory scheme (the famous triad of the high-priest, the king, and the prophet). Solovyov's political ideas in fact were not sufficiently thought out; there was something of the unpractical visionary about him, and he did not succeed in breaking finally with the traditions in which he had been brought up. But there is no organic connection between his philosophy and those of his political views which reactionaries love to interpret to their own advantage, invoking the authority of Solovyov's name to cover up their own dark designs. In any case, for me there is no doubt whatever that Slavophilism as a political conception is dead and will never come to life again; it must be completed by the westernizers' theory.

The same must be said about economic Slavophilism or the old 'populism' which has finally broken down before our eyes under the pressure of historical facts,[1] so that the recent sharp antithesis between Marxism and populism has now disappeared. Both of the political and of the economic Slavophilism we must say, *requiescat in pace*.

Solovyov has often been called, in earnest and in jest, a prophet, because of both his teaching and his appearance. His was indeed a prophetic office; he was misunderstood and laughed at by his contemporaries, but his value is more and more recognized as the years go by. Mankind has lived through many centuries of doctrinaire clericalism hostile to free thought and scientific inquiry; we are now living in an age of doctrinaire rationalism which has rejected first religion and now philosophy in the name of exact science and free inquiry. But there are grounds for thinking that this period too is coming to an end and that its positive potentialities are being exhausted. The time has come for a new, higher synthesis in which the inquiring spirit returns to itself, to its perennial quest and, enriched by the centuries-long development of thought and knowledge, frees itself from the domination of abstract principles taken in isolation and harmoniously combines them all. The quest for such a synthesis was Solovyov's life-work. In the dim twilight of existence we mistake for the source of light some objects which merely reflect it better than others. With the prophetic vision of a seer Solovyov perceived the true source—the light which is eternal and unfading. All his life he strove towards this light and called others to it. Let us follow him!

---

[1] It is only in one respect that the original position of Russian Marxism remains in force and needs no substantial emendations—namely, in understanding the economic development of Russia as a capitalistic process bound up with the development of industrialism.

3

Signposts: 1909

In 1909 a group of Russian intellectuals, members of the 'intelligentsia' and others, published a small volume of essays which were to prove of great historical importance. In it one may see reflected a new attitude towards Marxism, religion, and the future. Nicolas Berdyaev and Sergius Bulgakov were among the authors of the collection, which was entitled *Signposts*. The following essay from the symposium was Bulgakov's contribution. (*Vekhi* (Moscow, 1909), pp. 140 ff.)

Heroism and Otherworldliness

The most fundamental characteristic of the Russian intelligentsia is its attitude to religion. Without bearing this well in mind it is impossible to understand the essential character of the revolution of 1905. Russia's historical future too is bound up with the relation in which the intelligentsia is to stand towards religion. It may remain dead to it as before or there may be a radical change in this respect, a true revolution in heart and mind.

It has often been pointed out (following Dostoyevsky) that the typical mentality of the Russian intelligentsia has features in it which are religious, sometimes indeed almost Christian. These qualities were developed, in the first place, by its historical destiny: on the one hand by government persecutions which created in it a sense of being martyrs and confessors, and on the other by its enforced separation from practical life, resulting in day-dreaming, sometimes in idealistic sentimentality, utopianism, and generally speaking in a deficient sense of reality.

A certain unworldliness, eschatological dreams of the City of God, of the coming kingdom of righteousness (under various socialistic pseudonyms), and the striving to save humanity, if not from sin, at any rate from suffering, are the well-known invariable and distinguishing characteristics of the Russian intelligentsia. Pain at the disharmony of life and a longing to overcome it are characteristic of the best writers from among the intelligentsia (Gleb Uspensky, Garshin).[1] This striving for the 'City which is to come' by comparison with which earthly reality seems pale and dim shows perhaps in the most recognizable form features of the lost 'churchiness' that still remains among the intelligentsia. How often during the sittings of the Second Duma in the stormy speeches of the atheistic Left I

---

[1] Gleb Uspensky (1840–1902) was a writer of documentary novels and V. Garshin (1855–88) a short-story writer. Both lost their reason, and Garshin committed suicide.

detected, strange as it may seem, echoes of an Orthodox psychology, a sudden influence of its spiritual heritage!

Nevertheless, in spite of all this, it is well known that in no other country is the literate public so atheistic as in Russia. Atheism is the general faith into which all who enter the humanistic church of the intelligentsia are baptized, whether they come from the educated class or from the ranks of the people.

Rejecting Christianity and the norms of life laid down by it, our intelligentsia adopts together with, or rather as the positive side of, its atheism the religion of the deification of man in one of the forms developed in the western European 'enlightenment'. The basic dogma common to all its varieties is a belief in man's natural perfection, in endless progress realized by man's own powers, and at the same time a mechanistic interpretation of that progress. Since all evil is explained by the bad organization of human society, there is no such thing as personal guilt or personal responsibility; the whole task of social organization consists in overcoming these external imperfections, of course through similar external reforms. Denying Providence and any preordained plan which is being fulfilled in history, man puts himself in the place of Providence and regards himself as his own saviour.

Side by side with this antichrist principle there are in the Russian intelligentsia lofty religious possibilities, a new historical reality awaiting spiritual birth. The intensity with which it seeks the City of God and the longing for God's will to be done on earth as it is in heaven differ profoundly from the striving of bourgeois culture for secure earthly well-being. The ugly, misshapen, and impracticable maximalism of the the intelligentsia is the result of a religious travesty, but it may be overcome through religious regeneration.

The Russian intelligentsia is religious in its very nature. Dostoyevsky in *The Possessed*[1] compared Russia, and in the first instance its intelligentsia, to the Gadarene demoniac in the gospel possessed by many devils, who was healed by Christ alone and could only find health and recovery at the feet of the Saviour. This comparison holds good in our day too. A legion of devils has entered the Russian colossus and

[1] Published in 1871, its Russian title is *The Devils*.

is shaking it with convulsions, tormenting and crippling it. Only through religious achievement, great though invisible, can she be healed and freed from that legion. The intelligentsia has renounced Christ, turned away from his face, torn his image out of its heart, deprived itself of the inner light of life, and, together with its native land, is paying for this betrayal, for this religious suicide. But, strange to say, it cannot forget its heart-wound, recover its spiritual balance, and rest content with this self-wrought devastation. Having renounced Christ, it still bears his seal upon its heart and tosses about with unconscious longing for him, unable to quench its spiritual thirst. And this restless anguish, this other-worldly dream of other-worldly righteousness lays a peculiar stamp upon it, makes it strange, frenzied, unbalanced, as it were 'possessed'. It is like the beautiful Shulamite who lost her bridegroom; on her bed by night, in the streets and in the broad ways she sought him whom her soul loved; she asked the watchmen that go about the city if they had seen her beloved, but instead of answering her the watchmen smote her and wounded her.[1] And yet the Beloved, he for whom her soul is yearning, is so near. He is standing and knocking at this heart—the proud, rebellious heart of the intelligentsia. Will his knocking ever be heard?

---

[1] Song of Solomon 3.1–3, 5, 7.

4

Two Cities: 1911

Bulgakov saw the perennial Christian problem of the City of God and the cities of the earth as cast in a radically new light by the rise of Marxism. He may have been the first theologian to give systematic analysis of Karl Marx as a 'religious type'. The following two essays are taken from *Dva Grada*, first published in Moscow in 1911.

Karl Marx as a Religious Type

I believe that the determining power in man's spiritual life is his religion, both in the narrow and the wider sense of the term, i.e., the ultimate values which man recognizes as being *above* him and his practical relation to these values. To discover a man's real religious centre, to find his true spiritual core, means to learn the most intimate and important thing about him; and then everything external and derivative will be comprehensible. In this sense one may speak of every man having a religion, whether he be quite uncritical in his beliefs or consciously deny all definitely religious forms. Moreover, a Christian interpretation of life and history leaves no doubt that real mystical principles, mutually hostile and irreconcilable, dominate human minds and are a moving force in history. In this sense there are, strictly speaking, no religiously neutral people: in fact, a struggle between Christ and 'the prince of this world' is being waged in every heart.

We know that there may be people who do not know Christ but who serve him and do his will, and that those who call themselves Christians may in truth be alien to him. Both among unbelievers and among religious hypocrites there are men whose whole spirit foreshadows the deceiver destined to come 'in Christ's name' and to find many adherents. In reflecting upon the confusing phenomena of life, ever growing in complexity, one generally has to ask whose is the spirit that moves this or that historical figure, whose seal it is which is stamped on this or that historical movement. This question has to be asked again and again with reference to socialism, that highly complex, contradictory, and important current in the spiritual life of our time. The merely economic aims of socialism are not necessarily a matter of principle and need not give rise to theoretical doubts and arguments. The 'historical flesh' of socialism, i.e., the socialist movement, may at different times and places have different sources of inspiration and either belong to the kingdom of light or fall prey to darkness. There is a mysterious dividing line between light and darkness which, though ever in company, never mix.

In thinking of the religious nature of modern socialism one's mind automatically turns to the man whose spirit so profoundly affected the socialist movement that he must be regarded as one of its spiritual fathers—Karl Marx. Who was he? What was his religious nature? Which god did he serve by his life-work? What love and what hate set his heart aglow? The reader does not expect of course to receive a simple, conventional answer which could only satisfy, perhaps, zealous catechumens in Marxism—namely, that Marx was wholly made up of socialistic sentiments, that he loved and pitied the downtrodden workers and hated exploiters and capitalists, and that he wholeheartedly believed in the coming bright era of socialism.

If it were all as simple as that, there would of course be nothing more to be said. But it is not quite like that, and in any case is infinitely more complex and puzzling. To begin with, as far as Marx's own psychology is concerned, it seems to me highly doubtful whether such feelings as love, spontaneous compassion, and warm sympathy for human suffering had a prominent place in his inner life. It was not for nothing that his own father said in a letter to Marx in his student days, 'I wonder if your heart is in keeping with your head, with your abilities?' He must have felt some doubt about it. Unfortunately there is an almost complete absence of written testimony with regard to Marx's personality and his life-history. There are very few descriptions of his character by subtle and competent observers, not concerned to give a strictly 'social-democratic' account of him (as Lafargue and Liebknecht do). Accordingly, estimates of Marx's character are bound to be largely subjective. To judge by his published works, he was far more accessible to anger, hatred, and malice than the opposite kind of feelings. It is true that sometimes his anger was righteous, but often enough it was anything but righteous. Marx's words deserve every sympathy and respect when he thunders against the cruelty of capitalism and the capitalists, and the heartlessness of the social system of his day; but they call forth a different sort of reaction when, alongside the 'thunder', one finds haughty and vindictive attacks upon all who think differently, whether it be Lassalle or MacCullough, Herzen or Malthus, Proudhon or Senior. Marx readily entered into personal polemics, and it must be confessed that his polemics were distinctly objectionable— much as his supporters try to deny it. Marx wrote three polemical books (to say nothing of shorter writings), and it is painful to read them now, not merely because at all times polemics are of more interest to the writers than to the readers.[1]

It was Feuerbach, not Hegel, who gave Marx his starting-point, and the central place in Feuerbach's philosophy is occupied by the religious problem. Its main theme is the rejection of the religion of God-manhood in the name of the religion of man-godhead; it is anti-theistic, militant atheism. This was the keynote to which Marx's mind responded most fully; when Hegelianism broke up into a number of different schools, Marx's ear selected from all the abundance and variety of philosophical motifs resounding at that period the religious one of rebellion against God.

Feuerbach's work *Das Wesen des Christenthums* was published in 1841, and it produced such an impression upon Marx and Engels (according to the latter's account) that they both at once became Feuerbachians.[2]

Marx has indelibly stamped the socialist movement with his spirit, and consequently with the spirit of Feuerbach, of which in the religious and philosophical sphere he was the instrument. This spirit permeates the general conception of socialism worked out by Marx in accordance with the demands of militant atheism; it gives the tone to his whole system and turns socialism into a means of struggling against religion. The general historical problems of socialism may be clear enough, but the actual forms of the socialist movement can, as we know, differ greatly in spiritual content and moral value. They may be inspired by lofty, purely religious enthusiasm in so far as socialism seeks to realize righteousness, love, and justice in social relations; or by feelings of a different and by no means lofty kind: class hatred, selfishness, philistinism turned inside out—in short, all the feelings which under the

[1] Bulgakov, S. N., *Dva Grada* (Farnborough, Hants, 1971), pp. 3 ff.
[2] Ibid.

name of 'the class point of view' and 'class interests' play such
a leading part in Marxist preaching. Indignation against evil
is of course a noble and even a holy feeling that no vital social
worker can do without. And yet there is a fine, almost imperceptible but perfectly real dividing line beyond which this
holy feeling becomes anything but holy. The transition may
be easy, natural, and indeed unnoticeable, but the preponder-
ance of one or the other kind of feeling determines the spiritual
quality both of individuals and of the movement. In our
practical age, however, it is not usual to take an interest in
the inner aspect of things unless it has some direct practical
significance.

The whole of Marx's doctrine followed from his basic
religious motive: militant atheism. Economic materialism,
the preaching of class hatred, the denial of universally human
values and universally binding moral norms transcending
class interests, the concept of an impassable gulf that divides
the world of the proletariat with its lofty mission from the
'whole reactionary mass' of its exploiters—all these teachings
were, naturally, bound to coarsen the socialist movement, to
give it a more prosaic, earthly, and purely economic character.
Class hatred takes the place of universal human love. This was
certainly not due to the influence of Marx alone; the spiritual
temptation in question was too strong for the socialist movement even apart from Marx, and both before and after him
made itself felt in many different ways; but Marx was a
powerful instrument of it. Marx's personal influence in the
movement was mainly responsible for the intensification of
the anti-religious, militantly atheistic element which rages in
it, as it does in our civilization as a whole.

Vladimir Solovyov (1853–1900) showed a profound understanding of the true character of the anti-religious forces which
strive to entice the socialist movement and to gain possession
of it. In his 'Fable of the Antichrist'[1] he makes his Antichrist,
among other things, a socialist and social reformer.

In socialism, as all along the line in our civilization, a
struggle is going on between Christ and Antichrist.[2]

[1] Solovyov, V. S., *War and Christianity: Three Conversations* (London, 1915), pp. 144 ff.
[2] Bulgakov, S. N., op. cit., pp. 37 ff.

Two Cities

The success of socialism is, in the first place, a punishment for the sins of historical Christianity and a warning call to repentance. The strength of socialism testifies to some extent to the weakness of Christianity, which is losing its power over souls and giving way to another religion, another attitude to the world. I am far from thinking that the origin of the new religion could be entirely explained by those sins, since the consciousness of them might have called forth in fervent hearts a desire to combat them without in any sense deserting Christianity for the religion of man-worship. For such desertion to take place other forces, distinctly anti-Christian, had to come into play. But undoubtedly those sins prepared the ground for defection. This is particularly true of sins in the domain of social thought and action. In the Christian world the feeling of social duty, or so to speak of social love, was not sufficiently manifested; Christians relied too much on the old, traditional methods of social assistance (such as direct almsgiving), while remaining comparatively deaf to the voice of science and blind to historical changes in the social economy and capitalistic production. Various sinful propensities also played their part—greed, servility, indifference under the cloak of piety; the most precious beliefs were used as a means for self-justification or as a mask. As Ruskin put it, we generally believe in immortality so as to avoid preparing for death, and disbelieve in it so as to avoid preparing for a future life. Not infrequently the gospel texts about patience and abstinence are interpreted hypocritically and applied not to oneself but to others, especially to the poor.

The sins of historical Christianity in the social domain are great and numerous; they must not be passed over in silence but recognized so that they may be corrected, since a terrible hour of reckoning is at hand. Those sins are due not only to weakness or malice of will, but also to a one-sided interpretation of Christianity—to what might be called individualistic hyper-asceticism, which does away with the very idea of history and hence of historical tasks and duties. Attention is wholly centred upon the solitary life of the soul that has renounced the world and freed itself from participation in history. This comes to be regarded as the only normal form of Christian life; the world is abandoned to natural forces or to atheism, and the ground is thus cleared for socialism. Stern historical reality compels us, however, to consider its demands; a religious victory over socialism can only be won on the basis of a Christian philosophy of history, i.e., not by negative criticism alone but by developing the positive implications of Christianity.

Leaving aside these long-term views, we must say that in its direct historical significance the success of the materialistic religion of man-worship and its diffusion among the masses signals an approaching danger to culture, a menace to civilization, an insidious disease that is gradually undermining the spiritual health of mankind. It is often forgotten and by no means generally understood that our present civilization historically has its roots in religion and is still drawing healthy sap from them. People mistake the last page of history for the entire book, the flower for the whole plant, failing to see the inner bond between the past and the present, the organic succession of cultural development in its entirety. The new Europe has been spiritually nurtured and educated by the Christian Church, and modern European culture with its science and learning is Christian in origin, although it is beginning to forget this.

Not a single civilization in history has been built upon an atheistic foundation—and indeed, I am convinced, it cannot be. An atheistic culture can only be a parasite plant on an alien stock, and one that kills the tree upon which it is feeding. Self-deification is not a life-giving but a death-bringing principle. I admit that its introduction may make it easier to attain some particular historical purpose in the near future, just as a dose of poison may result in an unhealthy and short-lived access of energy. It is quite possible that by introducing the poison of materialistic man-worship into the people's soul we may hasten the movement of the proletariat against the capitalists, mobilize the social revolution, and force important social reforms. But what will be the price of this victory? What will be the spiritual powers of the people in the next historical epoch? Only those who believe in economic providence and in the omnipotence of elemental forces in history, who deny human personality, regarding it as a mere reflex, can lightly and confidently look into the future, oblivious of the odour of putrefaction rising from the people's soul deprived of the salt of Christianity. But in truth history is created by living forces and not by lifeless elements, and human personality with its ideals and its religion is the creative, constructive principle in history. Man is the son of eternity plunged into the stream of time, the son of freedom held captive by necessity and dependent upon the laws of nature, of the material, physical world. He creates history only in so far as he is free, and he is free in so far as he serves an ideal and rises above necessity, denying its power to determine him. But he destroys his freedom in so far as he sinks into the world of things and submits to their ruling power, which he is called upon to combat; only in struggling against it does he build up culture. It cannot with impunity be dinned into a man's ear that he is a two-legged brute, that his nature is purely animal, and that therefore the only thing left him is to recognize this and to worship his own brutishness. One cannot with impunity, in opposition to the centuries-long call of Christianity: 'Lift up your hearts', persuade men to lower them. One cannot deprive man of the ideal of personality and hide Christ's image from him without devastating his soul. The hidden roots of history go deep into the ground. The seed out of which the many-branched tree of European civilization has grown was early Christianity in all its indivisible simplicity. Without assuming the part of a Cassandra, one cannot help seeing that the lowering of ideals is a cultural and historical menace to the very sources of creativeness.

I will not deny that I feel a quite special anxiety at the thought of my own country and people, whose soul is still firmly bound up mystically and historically with early Christianity and is so near to it in its direct and simple faith. It too is exposed to the action of the parching wind which blows this time not from the East but from the West. Our country is going through a profound and far-reaching crisis

—political, economical, cultural—and all the thoughts and
efforts of the living members of the community are directed
towards healing its disease. It is not for me to belittle the
importance, the difficulty, and the vital significance of this
task; woe and shame to those who stand aside from it! But
the greatness and value of this reformative work and anxiety
for daily bread must not let us forget the people's soul, its
health and development, and the need to protect it from
demoralization and decay. If the soul of the people is cor-
rupted, we lose the foundation upon which the whole of
Russia's present and future is based—its political being,
national wealth, and national culture. Let us preserve for the
future ages the people's holy of holies—their heart, their
conscience, and their faith, set alight by a lamp in the catacombs. Then we shall not fear any historical trials, and
nothing will shake our faith in the future of a people which
by its sufferings made Russia great, but nurtured in its heart
a different and a higher ideal bequeathed to it by early
Christianity. True to that ideal, it named its fatherland *holy*
Russia![1]

[1] Bulgakov, S. N., op. cit., pp. 46–50.

5

Quiet Thoughts: 1918

Selections from *Tichie Dumy*, written in far from quiet times and published in 1918.

The Corpse of Beauty
(Upon viewing a Picasso exhibition)

The art of Matisse, Gauguin, Cezanne, Renoir, and others is like a brilliant day of which one wants to say with the poet: 'By the high will of the gods a gold-woven veil is thrown over the nameless abyss of the mysterious world of spirits. This brilliant veil is day, day that gives life to the earth-born, heals aching hearts, and is the friend of men and of gods.'[1] But when one enters the room where Pablo Picasso's works are collected, one is surrounded by an atmosphere of mystical fear amounting to terror. The veil of day with its reassuring multiplicity of colours is blown away, and one is encircled by horrible formless night, full of dumb, evil phantoms and shadows. It is stifling like the grave.

But the day fades, the night has come and flung away from the ill-fated world the cover of the gracious veil; and the abyss is laid bare before us with its fears and mists, and there are no more barriers between us and it. This is why night is fearful to us.[2]

Picasso's art is exactly such a moonless and starless night and just as mystical as it. This is true not of the subjects of his paintings (which, on the contrary, are quite ordinary and even trivial and are generally confined to women's figures, clothed or nude, and to still life) but of his brushwork, his colours, his whole technique; the very nature of his art is mystical throughout. It is certainly mystery-painting, even though it cannot be called religious, and there is, strangely enough, something of the ikon about it. In spite of the swift development and radical changes in Picasso's methods, the spiritual content of his art is all of a piece and from beginning

[1] Bulgakov's reference is to a poem entitled 'Day and Night' by Tyutchev. (Tyutchev, Th. I., *Stichotvoreniya* (Berlin, 1921), p. 102.) [Ed.]
[2] Ibid.

to end is permeated by one feeling of ever increasing anguish and horror of life. Unquestionably Picasso has strength, and he not merely tries to appear strong (as many do nowadays in Nietzsche's fashion), but his brush has real power. An 'exacting artist', he unremittingly works out the form corresponding to his idea and brings it to the utmost perfection; in thus labouring over form he shows the pertinacity of a great master. This young painter, a Spaniard by birth, with an admixture of Moorish blood (a very important feature!) has already passed through a long process of artistic development, the main phases of which can be seen in this gallery. His early pictures, painted with great skill and power in the ordinary realistic style (*The Drunkard,* two male portraits, *The Old Jew and a Boy, The Tryst,* etc.), are remarkable for the expression of acute, almost subhuman anguish in the eyes and a kind of music of desolation in the figures. Then follow the works of his later, Cubist period, which produce the most striking impression and are, up to the present, the culminating point of his art. Here is the pensive *Isabeau,* as it were fettered with misery; here is the mournful *Seated Woman* that wrings one's heart with pity; then there come truly demonic images. Here is the *Nude in a Landscape* twisted in a hideously erotic attitude. Her legs are like the flippers of a seal, she is fat, heavy, falling to pieces; the picture breathes cynical malice and is a wild challenge of depravity, dissolution, and decay. Here is the *Woman after a Dance* sitting heavily in an armchair and looking into the distance with malignant eyes; how well the disconnected blocks of paint are suited for depicting this vampïre with a body built only of malice and geometrical lines! Here is the *Lady with a Fan,* entirely made up of triangles and other geometrical figures, malignant, leering, and inhuman. Here are three women like nightmare visions painted in purplish flaming tints, heavily immobile in their dance. Here is the terrible *Farmer's Wife* made up of geometrical masses of stone, the embodiment of heaviness and inertia. The body has lost its warmth, vitality, and fragrance and become linear, geometrical, stony; life has been transfixed in a grimace, flesh has been sterilized and drained of blood with a sort of demonic asceticism. It is spirituality, but the spirituality of a vampire or a demon: passions, even the lowest of them, are taken in their purely spiritual, incorporeal essence: they are disincarnate. These pictures manifest quite a special, non-human method of seeing and perceiving flesh, an evil spiritualism disruptive of the flesh and full of hatred and contempt for it; and yet—such is the irony of things— the painter can speak only through the flesh and its imagery.

From the technical point of view, especially with regard to colour effects, the paintings of this second period are probably very remarkable. Their mystical power and content are equally striking; so much so that the paradoxical, deliberate hideousness of Cubist painting is soon forgotten, one simply ceases to notice it—a clear sign that the form perfectly fits its content and that in this sense the work is highly artistic. It is difficult to give an idea of Picasso's paintings without reproducing them in colour. Their main subject is unquestionably woman, the Feminine itself, artistically apprehended and perceived in different forms. How then does the painter see and feel this Feminine? This is the key to the understanding of his art, since the eternal Feminine, the world's soul, is the mother and mistress of all art. In Picasso's art she appears in unutterable humiliation as a hideous, heavy, shapeless, and decomposing body, indeed as the very corpse of beauty, seen in God-defying cynicism (*Nude in a Landscape*), in diabolical malice (*After the Dance*), as a decaying astral corpse (*Seated Woman*), or with the snake-like leer of a witch (*Woman with a Fan*). And all those visions live and are something like miracle-working ikons of a demonic nature; an uncanny power flows from them. To look at them for any length of time gives one a kind of mystical dizziness. They are so artistically convincing and mystically true that it is impossible to doubt for a moment the artist's sincerity and the mystical realism of his art. It is curious that the same powerful and uncanny impression is produced by his other pictures of the same period in spite of their wholly inoffensive subjects: still life, a bottle and a tumbler, a vase of fruit. It is the same unredeemed, hopeless heaviness, the same mystic dread and anguish. A kind of dark force emanates from them all and makes itself almost tangibly felt. These powerful and eerie 'black ikons' actually remind one of some Egyptian idols of sacred animals (in the Egyptian section of the Emperor

Alexander III Museum). What hell there must be in the artist's soul if its expressions are of this kind! His paintings give one a nightmare. There is not a single ray of light in this arid and sorrowful desert, scorched by the flames of hell. The favourite colours of Picasso's palette, by the way, used by him to perfection, are purplish red and muddy orange— colours of evil significance in the 'aura'.

I do not clearly understand the meaning and value of Picasso's recent paintings, confined mostly to still life in a disintegrated form. Does it mean a special kind of perception in four-dimensional space and its projection on a surface? Or is it a case of 'occult clairvoyance', of images from other planes of being, so that their pictorial representation is related to the original in the same way as a musical score is related to sound? Is it decay, or a higher state of art? Unquestionably Picasso introduces into a flat representation rhythms of movement inaccessible to ordinary vision (as Churlanis does in his pictures). It is impossible to doubt the truth and sincerity of this latest stage of Picasso's development, but since its meaning is not clear to me, I speak here only of the Picasso of yesterday—of his first and particularly of his second period.

The impression produced by Picasso's work is one of the most powerful that art can give, though it is qualitatively different from that given by the great works of antiquity or of the Renaissance (for instance by the Venus de Milo or the Sistine Madonna). There is something in it that makes it 'modern', characteristic of our spiritual epoch; this is why it is so suggestive, provocative, and disturbing. It is not easy to analyse the chaos that rises from the depths of the psyche, from the 'nocturnal consciousness'.[1]

The mystical nature of art is here laid bare and made self-evident. This is why after Picasso everything else in the same gallery, though masterpiece it may be, somehow falls flat and seems insipid, naïve, unconscious. *Mir gab der Gott sagen was ich leide*—this applies to every true artist, and it has been given to Picasso to confess the unknown and mysterious noumenal sin through which he has become the plaything of an obsessing spirit, an artistic, and therefore convincing *advocatus diaboli*. Accordingly, Picasso's art is a powerful

[1] Bulgakov, S. N., *Tichie Dumy* (Moscow, 1918), pp. 33–7.

religious temptation, a trial of faith. Demonism in art is of course the most subtle, intimate, and therefore dangerous form of Luciferian infection in human creativeness, since art, in contradistinction to philosophy and even more to science, is connected with the inmost depths of the spirit. One may not know Picasso, or one may ignore him through spiritual laziness, indolence, or for moral and ascetic reasons, since unquestionably his is a morbid art. But it is not always possible or indeed right to do so, just as it would not be right in reading *The Brothers Karamazov* to skip the pages on rebellion and pass at once to Zossima. It is not easy to tackle in earnest Picasso's representation of the world and to overcome it.[1] He is frightening because he is demonically genuine. Possession is once more becoming prevalent; struggle with it requires sobriety, spiritual health, integration of personality, and above all the rock of faith, reliance not upon our solitary and subjective selves but upon the 'togetherness'[2] of the Church. Only in the name of Christ within the Church can demons be exorcised.

There exists a mysterious rhythm, a certain musical correlation between light and darkness, in obedience to which the unknown architect of Notre Dame in Paris placed on its outer balustrade his *chimères*, demonic monsters of great artistic power and profound mystical reality. I have always marvelled at the riddle of the *chimères*, those demons that have settled on the roof of the cathedral: what anguish wrung them from the artist's heart? To how many men have they been a temptation and a stumbling block? I mean not the Baedeker-led tourists, but those who gathered under the roof of the beautiful cathedral to pray, both in the far-off Middle Ages and in our own day. Are not Picasso's paintings also *chimères* on the spiritual temple of modernity? It is impossible to imagine these evil things inside the cathedral; if Picasso's pictures were brought into a church one fancies they would, like the *chimères*, be immediately burnt up and turn to ashes. And yet, in virtue of some mysterious attraction, those

[1] Dostoyevsky makes Prince Myshkin in *The Idiot* say of Holbein's *Descent from the Cross*: 'This picture might cause some people to lose faith!' A similar thing might be said of Picasso's paintings.

[2] *Sobornost* [Ed.].

DBA

unclean spirits settle on the roof of a church. It is remarkable, too, that so many motifs in Picasso's art go back to African idols which his African ancestors may have worshipped; thus his *chimères* are hieratic in their very derivation.

There remains another question, unanswerable and enigmatic: was the majestic portal of the Paris Cathedral the work of the same artist as the *chimères*, or of two quite different men? History does not say.[1]

---

[1] Bulgakov, S. N., op. cit., pp. 50ff.

A Professorial Religion

In *Three Conversations* Solovyov has given an artistic image of Protestantism in the person of Professor Pauli as the representative of critical inquiry into Christianity. Catholicism and Orthodoxy are represented respectively by Pope Peter II and 'the Elder' John, and the spirit of Protestantism is embodied in a university professor who, at the last moment of history, after centuries of study and doubt, says about the basic truths of Christianity: *'Jetzt ist es ja gründlich erwiesen und ausser jedem Zweifel gesetzt.'* And indeed if it be asked what is the inmost religious core of Protestantism, the answer will have to be that it is the science of theology, the service of God through faithful and honest research into objective historical truth. In Protestantism professors of theology are the highest and indeed the only ecclesiastical authority. They are the teachers of faith and the guardians of Church tradition, which before our eyes has become a scientific tradition or an historical science.

Protestantism is in this sense a professorial religion. I say this with neither irony nor admiration and simply state an historical fact. It is both very much and extraordinarily little. It is very much because in our age science plays a tremendous part in life and has put its stamp upon every aspect of the modern mind. Religious problems must also inevitably pass through the crucible of science; in a certain sense religion itself (to say nothing of philosophy) is becoming scientific and therefore those who are masters of this science obtain tremendous power over human minds and influence the people's religious life. And practically the whole of modern exegesis has been nurtured by Protestantism; critical religious thought of our day is spiritually dependent upon it, with all its strong and weak points. It cannot be said of course that this science does not exist outside Protestantism, but throughout the nineteenth century and down to the present day, the Protestant countries (and in the first instance of course

Germany) have played the leading part in it. New incentives have come from there, systematic collective work of real value is going on apace. But this is all that there is—inwardly and mystically—in Protestantism as pure 'service of the word' in its modern form. And this is extraordinarily little for religion. Morbid individualism and intellectualism are in Protestantism not overcome through the reality of the Church; instead the living tradition of the Church is replaced more and more by historical science, the Church by a religious society, the sacraments and mystical worship by conventional symbolism. *Sobornost*—togetherness—is lost through a separation between the learned and the ignorant; the experience of spiritual life is replaced by a university seminar; and the place of the saints is taken by learned theologians. Protestantism has no ideal of holiness and no path to it, and without this there is no true religion, just as there is no art without artistic genius. Protestantism carries on its world-wide religious mission, embodying the inquiring spirit of the unbelieving (or of the conscientiously doubting) Thomas, but it pays dearly for its service.

From the very beginning Protestantism contained an inner contradition which has become fully apparent in its history and determined its inner life. Luther and the Reformers forsook the Church and rejected its living traditions based upon faith in its mystical unity and communal reason; but they preserved the written part of this tradition, i.e., the Bible. As a literary monument it was made the basis of their doctrine, but it inevitably became the subject of critical inquiry, the ways and methods of which grew more and more complex. Hence the question of the divine inspiration of the Bible (*Inspirationsbegriff*) is of paramount importance to Protestantism, and in modern times the view that the Bible is merely a literary monument like any other has gained the upper hand. From the point of view of purely scientific inquiry it cannot be otherwise; but even the extremest representatives of Protestantism are not prepared to renounce the old, religious significance of the Bible. This can best be seen from the exclusive attention they devote to it. The study of the Bible still remains theology in the same sense as it was in Luther's time. It is in this necessity to combine a religious, i.e., certainly a non-scientific attitude to the Bible with its scientific interpretation, that the inner difficulty of Protestantism lies. It exists for all religious consciousness of the present day, but in Church Christianity, relying upon the living tradition, it cannot be as acute as in Protestant, purely biblical faith.

This is the source of its ceaseless inner restlessness and perpetual search for new paths—of the continuing Reformation which by no means ended with Luther. The German mind may justly be proud of its biblical science. After the flowering of German classical idealism it has produced nothing more imposing than the scientific study of religion, to which the finest scholarship of Germany is now devoted. One cannot but marvel at its scholarly, methodical discipline and industry. But characteristically enough, there is not a spark of genius in it, for genius has no place in this work, which is after all of only a relative and conditional value.[1]

The significant symptoms of religious self-consciousness in modern Protestantism are an additional illustration of our main thesis that Christianity can only exist as a Church or not at all. Modern Protestantism embodying the principle of individualistic Churchless Christianity is dissolving before our eyes in spite of every effort to save it, in spite of all the sincerity, learning, and profundity of its individual representatives. What is now taking place in it is of profound religious significance and deserves serious attention. Christianity exists only in the living, concrete Church tradition, apart from which there is merely the study of Christianity and remnants of the past, which the Reformation has inherited from the Church. Of course, not even Church dogma is a defence against the poison of modern scientific doubt. The question as to the religious significance of critical inquiry and its rights and limits exists within the Church too, though in a different setting, but there science is not regarded as the final criterion of religious truth.

In one way or another, the problem of the Church is becoming more and more acute through the mere force of circumstance, through the actual development of learning and religious philosophy. In this worldwide movement of thought

[1] Bulgakov, S. N., *Tichie Dumy*, pp. 146 ff.

great merit attaches to Protestantism with its scholarship and its intellectual conscience; its merits are great, even when it bears witness to the. truth only through a. consistent revelation of error.[1]

---

[1] Ibid., pp. 162 ff.

6

Doctrinal Works: 1926–44

In one sense, most of Father Bulgakov's work was doctrinal in character. The selection which follows is taken from his specifically systematic writings, published after his exile from Russia.

St Peter and St John

The study of the relevant New Testament texts proves that St Peter really had the first place among the twelve apostles; though it was a priority not of power but of authority, seniority, primacy which only belonged to him in conjunction with all the others and not apart from or without them. Peter was indeed first among apostles, in accordance with Christ's choice and preordination, and his priority cannot be denied. It must, however, be put within proper limits, to begin with in a personal sense. Peter has priority among the twelve as their head and representative; he is called and proclaimed by Christ, who singled out Peter by word and deed and named him. But beside the twelve there came to be a thirteenth apostle, who was not there when Peter made his confession near Caesarea Philippi and did not dine with Christ and his disciples by the sea of Tiberias, and therefore did not hear the threefold charge to 'Feed my sheep'. He was chosen and made an apostle by Christ himself, so to speak, outside Peter's province and without any relation to him, and he laid great emphasis on this election: 'Paul, an apostle (not of men, neither by man, but by Jesus Christ and God the Father)' (Gal. 1.1); 'a servant of Jesus Christ, called to be an apostle, separated unto the Gospel of Christ' (Rom. 1.1); 'I neither received the gospel of man, neither was I taught it, but by the revelation of Jesus Christ' (Gal. 1.12). 'When it pleased God, who separated me from my mother's womb and called me by His grace to reveal His Son in me, that I might preach Him among the heathen; immediately I conferred not with flesh and blood; neither went I up to Jerusalem to them which were apostles before me' and only 'after three years I went to Jerusalem to see Peter' (Gal. 1.15–18) and 'then fourteen years after I went up again to Jerusalem by revelation' to see the apostles and get James, Cephas, and John, 'who seemed to be pillars' to recognize that 'the gospel of the uncircumcision was committed unto me, as the gospel of the circumcision was unto Peter' (Gal. 2.7–10; cf. 1 Cor. 9–11; 2 Cor. 11.5).

It is indisputable that although St Paul was not out of contact or agreement with the twelve, he had autonomy and affirmed his independence of 'Peter and those with him'. 'Am I not an apostle? Am I not free? Have I not seen Jesus Christ Our Lord?' (1 Cor. 9.1). Paul has a vivid and, one may say, militant sense of his apostolic freedom and autonomy, and all his work is in fact carried on quite independently of other apostles. '. . . In nothing am I behind the very chiefest apostles' (2 Cor. 12.11). It would be strange and erroneous to affirm that Paul too was somehow bound by Peter's primacy while he himself felt that he was not bound by anything. Paul was, so to speak, extra-territorial to Peter or the twelve: Paul is on one side, the apostles are on the other. The new 'founder of Christianity' does his great work, obeying direct suggestions from above and the behests of his own conscience. In relation to the twelve he is not the thirteenth but the only one; Peter does not represent him, and Peter's primacy does not extend to him. Paul's preaching marks the first boundary of Peter's primacy. And Providence decreed that they should both be primates of the Church of Rome where they suffered martyrdom. Thus, the primacy of Peter in the first place where it was directly and most clearly manifested proved in fact not to be absolute, for it found its limit in Paul. This is also borne out by the fact that from of old the Church, Eastern and Western alike, has celebrated together the memory of the holy and chief apostles Peter and Paul. The Church prepares the faithful for the celebration of these twin apostles of Rome by a common fast. The significance of this celebration, as interpreted in the church services (for 29 and 80 June), makes it impossible to regard the commemoration of Peter and Paul as the feast in honour solely of St Peter's primacy. The words of the service most decidedly affirm the headship of Peter, but at the same time assert the headship of Paul as well, in such terms that their pre-eminence does not bring them into conflict, but they are seen to be mutually complementary. One of the *Kathismata*[1] hymns at Matins actually declares them 'equal in grace and rank'.

---

[1] 'The Apostles' Lent', the length of which varies with the date of Easter, since it begins a week after Whit Monday. There is also 'Our Lady's Lent', 1–14 August, and St Philip's, 15 November to 24 December.

Turning to the Gospel according to St John, we must observe that in its general aim it is complementary to the Synoptics and, coming as it does from one of the apostles closest to Christ, tells us something about that apostle himself. As one who witnessed and took part in the events related by him, he is bound to speak of himself; the Gospel *according* to John is also the Gospel *about* John. And indeed it gives a different picture of him, not of course in any way contradicting the Synoptics, but introducing quite new features into it. It shows the figure of John as the first among the apostles or a chief apostle alongside Peter, and this must in the end be clearly recognized. This is not a thesis put forward by an author determined to force it upon the reader (a '*Tendenz*'), but a conclusion which follows of itself from the contents of the Gospel according to John. We can mentally reproduce some of the unsolved and puzzling questions which were rife at the time when this Gospel was written; these questions found no answer in the Synoptics, being concerned with events subsequent to them. The main fact was that John was the only one of Christ's apostles still left on earth. The Mother of God's Assumption had taken place; Peter, the first of the apostles, had glorified God by his death. In what relation, then, did St John stand to his predecessors? There were mysterious rumours that the son of thunder should not taste death, especially when it proved to have no power over him in Rome, where both St Peter and St Paul had suffered martyrdom.[1] The theological content of St John's Gospel is a denunciation of docetism and an answer to questions connected therewith; with regard to problems of the Church's inner life it develops the conception of apostolic primacy, in particular with relation to John. It is in this sense that we must interpret what is said and left unsaid in St John, and also the manner in which it is said or passed over in silence.[2]

The two, Peter and John, after receiving Mary Magdalene's message, go to the sepulchre, and it is mentioned twice, evidently as a fact worth mentioning (and at the same time known only to an eyewitness) that John was the first to

---

[1] There is a legend that in the reign of Domitian John was miraculously saved from death in boiling oil.

[2] Bulgakov, S. N., *Svv. Pyotr i Ioann* (Paris, 1926), pp. 49 ff.

arrive, for he 'did outrun Peter' but for some reason did not go in. Peter, now free from fear, showed his usual impulsiveness and went into the sepulchre first, and John came in after him. But the remarkable thing is that only John believed. Even Peter's primacy in the affirmation of faith, which secured to him the promise about 'the rock', in this instance passes to John.[1]

Attention must also be drawn to the pair, Peter and John, as they are shown in Acts after Christ's Ascension and Pentecost. They appear together on only three occasions in Acts, but they are very important occasions. The first is the healing of the lame man, the first apostolic miracle after Pentecost.[2] Acts 3.1-4: 'Peter and John went up together into the temple at the hour of prayer, being the ninth hour . . . [the lame man] seeing Peter and John about to go into the temple asked an alms. And Peter fastening his eyes upon him with John said: Look upon us.' It is remarkable that they appear and act as a pair, though Peter speaks for both, and it is he who works the actual miracle of healing, anticipated by the commanding look of both (Acts 3.5-8); the healed man himself attributes the miracle not to Peter alone, who actually wrought it, but to the two together: 'And as the lame man which was healed held Peter and John, all the people ran together unto them in the porch that is called Solomon's' (Acts 3.11)—after which, as on the day of Pentecost, it is St Peter who begins to preach, thus manifesting his primacy.[3]

When in John 21.21 Peter asks: 'Lord, and what of this man?', in the Lord's reply John is not made subordinate to Peter: 'What is that to thee?' It is enough for him to look after himself: 'Follow thou me' (John 21.22). The primacy of John is the limit of Peter's primacy: there is not one but two primacies, or rather it is one, but a twofold, composite primacy. John reassures his flock in Asia Minor in their apprehensions. The Lord himself has circumscribed his domain, not allowing even the chief apostle Peter to interfere

---

[1] Ibid., p. 73.

[2] The other two instances are the testimony before the council in chapter 4, and the encounter with Simon Magus during the mission to Samaria in chapter 8.

[3] Bulgakov, S. N., op. cit., pp. 81 ff.

with it. By way of 'proof from the contrary' let us suppose that the words 'what is that to thee?' were not there. What a support this would give to the zealots of Peter's exclusive primacy! They would have a perfect right to conclude that the prince of the apostles thus clearly extends his 'universal care' as *episcopus universalis* to the beloved disciple and has the Saviour's support in this, since he answers Peter's question inspired by fatherly care. This, however, is not the case, and the question inspired either by curiosity or by 'care' is left unanswered.[1]

A grand and solemn testimony to John's primacy as an apostle is his Apocalypse, the revelation that was given him. John is a New Testament prophet among the apostles and the only apostle who was a prophet. He is indeed the only prophet of the New Testament, and his word, so to speak, sets a seal upon it. Apostle and prophet, he is the fellow-servant of the Angel of the Lord who showed him the mysteries: 'And I John saw these things, and heard them. And when I had heard and seen, I fell down to worship before the feet of the angel which showed me these things. Then saith he unto me, see thou do it not, for I am thy fellow-servant, and of thy brethren the prophets, and of them which keep the sayings of this book: worship God' (Rev. 22.8–9). And in a preceding passage: 'And I fell at his feet to worship him. And he said unto me, see thou do it not: I am thy fellow-servant and of thy brethren that have the testimony of Jesus: worship God; for the testimony of Jesus is the spirit of prophecy' (Rev. 19.10). The revelation given to John through the angel is 'the Revelation of Jesus Christ, which God gave unto him, to show unto his servants things which must shortly come to pass; and he sent and signified it by his angel unto his servant John' (Rev. 1.1–2). John appears as not only the witness and guardian of God's mysteries, but as the head of the seven churches in Asia (by accommodation these seven churches may be taken to represent the various forms of universal Christianity, and the destinies of Christ's Church in the world —corresponding to the number of spirits by his throne, the seven golden candlesticks, and the seven gifts of the Holy Spirit). To these seven churches, and through them to the

[1] Bulgakov, S. N., op. cit., p. 79.

universal Church as a whole, *urbi et orbi,* John sends his apostolic blessing: 'Grace be unto you and peace, from Him which is, and which was, and which is to come; and from the seven Spirits which are before His throne, and from Jesus Christ' (Rev. 1.4–5). John has the destinies of the Church revealed to him—not only of the Eastern Churches whose head he indisputably was, but of the universal Church at all times till Christ's second advent and the new heaven and new earth and the coming of the heavenly Jerusalem. To be chosen as the recipient of the revelation—even if the recipient were not Christ's beloved disciple—is to be raised to the highest rank of prophetic apostleship, and in John's case it crowns the primacy accorded to him during the Saviour's life on earth. Let us suppose for an instant that the revelation was given to Peter and not to John: what striking evidence this would have provided for the primacy of Peter! It would be said that he who was entrusted with the care and administration of the Church as a whole was also entrusted with the know-ledge of its future destinies. But then it may equally be said of John that his primacy was confirmed by the fact that the revelation was given to him. The significance of this fact, however, should be interpreted solely in the light of what we already know about John (and about Peter) from the gospel. The fact of the revelation does not as such establish apostolic primacy but bears witness to it and must be understood as its manifestation and confirmation. And, *vice versa,* absence of revelation in the case of the first apostle Peter testifies that Peter's primacy is that of high-priesthood but does not include prophecy, and therefore implicitly stops short of it. In any case there are no grounds for regarding it, with the Roman Catholic theologians, as the fullness of all the offices— the high priestly, the royal, and the prophetic, if only because this contradicts the fact that the revelation was given to St John alone.

At the same time, another difference between the two types of apostolic primacy is brought to light. Priesthood is in the order of succession both in the Old and in the New Testament Churches. Prophetic office, on the contrary, is individual and is not handed down in succession. And indeed if it be admitted that the beloved disciple has not tasted common human death and in some unknown way remains, succession is both superfluous and impossible, for he himself invisibly feeds his flock, prophetically inspiring it. At any rate, these are the surmises that suggest themselves upon consideration of all the relevant data.[1]

---

[1] Ibid., pp. 86–90.

The Friend of the Bridegroom

St John the Baptist was the first human being, after the Fall, who repented of Adam's sin and was ready for salvation, ripe for the Kingdom of God. He transferred his centre from himself to God; he alienated himself from his own self and thereby became fit to be the friend of the Bridegroom. And his soul entered into the joy of this friendship, as testified by the fiery words of the fourth Gospel: 'The friend of the bridegroom which standeth and heareth him, rejoices greatly because of the bridegroom's voice: this my joy therefore is fulfilled' (John 3.29).

This joy of the friend of the Bridegroom is the joy of every Christian soul at the approach of Christ, to whom it consecrates its human nature. It was given to John to accomplish his unique, personal service in his earthly life as the forerunner, and his achievement as prophet, preacher of repentance, and Baptist is, of course, absolutely unrepeatable. And yet it has a universally human significance and universally Christian content which is inevitably experienced by every man on his way to Christ—namely, penitence and self-renouncing love, the love proper to the friend of the Bridegroom. To be chosen to escort the heavenly Bridegroom to bring home his bride, his own human nature, a man must be in his heart the Bridegroom's friend.[1]

There are two types of the soul's relation to Christ as the Bridegroom. Every soul in the Church, giving itself to Christ and living his life, stands in the relation of 'bride' to him—like the Church itself, which receives its life of grace from him; this is the 'feminine' way of yielding to Christ. But there is also another way—if not of communion with, then at any rate of living for Christ, namely, our human, moral relation to

[1] The Forerunner is called 'brideleader' (*nymphagogos*) in hymns and prayers, though like the words *nymphentes* (groomsman) and *paranymphias* (best man) this does not occur in the New Testament. St John's phrase covers all and exactly defines the last.

him which consists in self-renunciation out of love for Christ. Then the soul learns the sweetness of friendship for the Bridegroom, the path of the Forerunner. This is the type of love between man and man, a 'masculine' relation to the Bridegroom. These two types are not mutually exclusive but form a composite and indivisible unity. Love is both self-renunciation and communion, as life in another; love is the unity of two in one life. The Church as the Bride of Christ has and gives this unity and communion of life, which is the principle of divine motherhood as expressed by the Church. The Church as a multiple unity of persons, after the image of the tri-Personal unity of God, consists in continual self-renunciation, dying for the sake of another, friendship with the Bridegroom. Love is sacrificial self-immolation and resurrection, union and friendship. The fullness of love and communion with Christ in the Church includes two aspects of love for Christ, of which one is appropriate to the office of Our Lady, the other to that of the Forerunner, the two figures who together stand beside the Saviour in the ikon called *Deēsis* ('Supplication').

This is why the Forerunner is not one among other saints revered by the Church, but has a unique significance. He cannot be compared even to the apostles, not even to the highest among them. The Lord trained them while he was on earth, preparing them for apostleship, struggling against their limitations and sometimes against their sinful weaknesses. Nevertheless, before the crucifixion they all lost heart and left him, remaining in misery and confusion until he appeared to them after his resurrection and until the pouring forth of the gifts of the Holy Spirit. The Forerunner begins his ministry when completely ready for it, having reached perfect maturity. He runs his course without the slightest stain or shadow of sin; he is the light of highest holiness accessible to man before Christ. The greatest of all born of woman, he is the highest of men in their human nature. Beside him stands only the Virgin Mary, who as the Mother of God is the highest of all creatures and therefore higher than he. In her human nature, however, in her human holiness, she is more akin to the Forerunner than to anyone else. This kinship consists in the absence of voluntary personal sin, in personal sinlessness, which of course does not mean freedom from original sin, from which only the Saviour can free human beings. (This is why the least in the Kingdom of God is greater than the greatest of those born of woman: human nature as such is weak and insufficient for salvation.) The Church significantly couples the Baptist with our Lady by celebrating after Christmas Day (on 26 December) the *Synaxis* (literally, assembly) of our Lady, and after Epiphany (on 7 January) the *Synaxis* of St John the Baptist,[1] for they are the chief human ministers in the Nativity and the Baptism of Christ respectively.

This unquestionably testifies to another thing: the achievement of the Forerunner is by no means annulled by the New Testament, but belongs to the essence of New Testament piety. Just like divine motherhood it abides as a foundation of Church life, revealing the human aspect or precondition of communion with God. John stands on the boundary between the Old and the New Testament, the old and the new man; he *is* that boundary: in him or through him the boundary is crossed in the human soul. That which once happened in him and to him is happening in the human heart to this day.

Thus the Forerunner together with the Mother of God remains in special, unmatched nearness to Christ the Saviour. They stand beside him on his ikons—and only these two, the Mother of God and the Forerunner, the mysterious pair representing the whole of mankind in its highest holiness and devotion to God.[2] And the place of this pair at the head of mankind is most strikingly and significantly indicated by the fact that as a rule the images of the Mother of God and the Forerunner appear on the sacred chalice, the receptacle of the Lord's precious and life-giving blood; medallions with their images are set on either side of that representing Christ the Lord. The Forerunner's particular nearness to the Lord could not be more profoundly and forcibly expressed. It was

[1] The *Synaxarion* is an assembling of non-biblical chapters, commemorating the saints or the mysteries, read at Matins. The feast of SS Peter and Paul is followed by a *Synaxis* of the twelve apostles, Lady Day by a *Synaxis* of the archangel Gabriel. [Ed.].

[2] The same order is attested in such documents of Western tradition as the *Confiteor* and the All Saints hymn *Jesu, Salvator saeculi* (translated by T. A. Lacey as No. 249 in *The English Hymnal*)—a kind of *Deēsis* in verse.

given him to touch with his right hand 'the head of Him whom he baptized'; it is given him, in and through his image, always to touch and to stand by the precious blood of the 'Lamb of God who taketh away the sin of the world'—the Lamb whom he himself had proclaimed and preached to the world.[1]

[1] Bulgakov, S. N., *Drug Zhenikha* (Paris, 1927), pp. 26 ff.

The Burning Bush

The Mother of God is the glory of the world, the world glorified in and for God, having God in itself and giving birth to him. We must grasp the full ontological significance of this and be perfectly clear about the theological implications and the dogmatic meaning of venerating her who is called 'more honourable than the Cherubim and incomparably more glorious than the Seraphim'.[1] The glory of the created world is made manifest in the glory of our Lady. The Mother of God is a personal revelation of the divine Wisdom, *Sophia*, which in another sense is Christ, 'the power and the wisdom of God'.[2] Thus there are two personal forms of *Sophia*: the created and the divinely human, and two human forms in heaven—the God-man and the Mother of God. This should be understood in connection with the doctrine of the Holy Trinity, of God and the world. The divine 'image'[3] in man is in heaven revealed and realized as the form of two: of Christ and of his Mother. The Son of God contains all the fullness of Godhead, inherent in the whole of the consubstantial and indivisible Holy Trinity. He also is the eternal man, prefigured in Adam, who as the new Adam is incarnate and becomes man. It is only on the basis of ontological kinship between the image and the archetype, the copy and its pattern, that the divine incarnation is possible, and the second Person of the Godhead can manifest himself as man. The character of man as the copy of God and the character of God as the pattern of man are shown, the one in the first, and the other in the second Adam. And yet there is another human form in heaven, like-wise near akin to the undiminished archetype of mankind—the Mother of God, 'the second Eve'. The first Eve was created

---

[1] In a hymn from the Liturgy of St John Chrysostom.
[2] 1 Cor. 1.24.
[3] Gen. 1.26–7. The Hebrew *selem* suggests the *cutting out*, as of a pattern; the Greek *ikon* and Latin *imago* imply tracing or following an outline. The Russian word is *obraz*.

out of the first Adam's rib. She could only have come into being in connection with him, as his necessary completion and revelation; the divine image in man was fully revealed only in the two (Gen. 1.27: 'God created man in His own image; in the image of God created He him; male and female created He them'). The first Adam and the first Eve are alike God's creation, though there is established between them an 'order of seniority': 'Adam is of God'[1] and Eve is of Adam. The second 'last' Adam is the Lord himself, who created both the flesh which he assumed and the second Eve, from whom he took it—a human being belonging to the created world.[2] In this sense she springs from the second Adam, as her creator, although she, as his Mother, gives him human flesh.[3] Further, Christ is the human expression of the second divine Person of the Godhead, the Logos. There is no direct human expression of the first person, for God the Father is revealed in his only-begotten Son, and only in and through him manifests himself to the world and to men. But in his personal being the Father is transcendent. (This is why it has been questioned whether it is right to represent him in a human image on the ikons of the Holy Trinity, even if it be as the Ancient of Days. Of course an ikon of God the Father as such, apart from the Holy Trinity, i.e., apart from his relation to the incarnate Son, is absolutely unthinkable.) But the Father reveals himself not only in the Son who is born of him, but also in the Holy Spirit, who proceeds from him and acts in the world from its very beginning. He 'moved upon the face of the waters' in the Old Testament, 'spoke through the prophets', anointed kings and hallowed the Old Testament Church. Later he descended upon the holy apostles and so upon every creature in the New Testament. Does the Holy Spirit also have a human expression? Is there a personal incarnation of him?

The Holy Spirit reveals himself to the creature through his action and his gifts only. His representations are obviously symbolical and do not reveal his person: He appears 'in a bodily shape like a dove' or in the vision of 'cloven tongues like as of fire', or in the likeness of one of the three angels seen

---

[1] Luke 3.38. Cf. 1 Cor. 11.3–12.
[2] 1 Cor. 15.45–9.   [3] 1 Cor. 11.12.

by Abraham[1] (and the three are not there distinguished). There is no personal, human incarnation of the third Person of the Trinity. But although the third Person is not personally incarnated as a human being in the same sense as the Son of God was, there is that one human, created personality which is the vessel filled by the Holy Spirit. She so completely surrendered her human, personal life as to make it transparent to the Holy Spirit, testifying about herself, 'Behold the handmaid of the Lord.' This being—the Blessed Virgin—is not the personal incarnation of the Holy Spirit but becomes his personal, living receptacle, an absolutely Spirit-bearing creature, a Spirit-bearing human being. For although there is no personal incarnation of the Spirit, there may be such a thing as personal Spirit-bearing, in which a created personality is completely surrendered in its createdness and is, as it were, dissolved in the Holy Spirit. This interpretation by the Spirit amounts to a change of kind. The Virgin is wholly deified, full of grace, 'a living temple of God'. Such a Spirit-bearing personality radically differs from the God-man, for she is a creature, but she differs as radically from the creation in its createdness, for she is raised and united to the divine life. And through this spiritualization is realized the image of God in man. It must therefore be admitted that in heaven[2] the human figure of the Mother of God, together with that of the God-man Jesus, jointly manifest the integral pattern of man. The ikon of our Lady and her Child, the Logos and the creature receiving him and filled with the Holy Spirit, in indivisible unity forms the pattern of man in his integrity. The God-man and the Spirit-bearer, the Son and the Mother, manifesting the revelation of the Father through the Word and Spirit, manifest the fullness of God's copy in man, or, the other way round, of the pattern of man in God.[3]

In iconography our Lady is not always depicted with the Child, as the Mother, but sometimes simply as the Virgin: such for instance is the ikon called *Umilenie* (The Tenderness), before which St Seraphim always prayed, the ikon called

[1] As in the well-known ikon by Andrei Rublev.
[2] As on the *ikonostas* (the chancel screen) of an Orthodox church, where these two figures flank the Royal Doors.
[3] Bulgakov, S. N., *Kupina Heopalimaya* (Paris, 1927), pp. 137–42.

Stena Nerushimaya (The Impregnable Defence), and others. These ikons represent the idea of the Bride rather than that of the Mother of God. This is in keeping with the facts that both in iconography and in Church hymns and patristic literature the Bride of the Song of Songs is sometimes identified with the Mother of God (see 1.8–16; 2.2–10; 3.6, 4; 4.9). The whole of the second half of Psalm 45 is taken to refer to her; the Song of Songs colours the special hymns for our Lady's festivals, and Psalm 45.9 is said when taking the particle from 'our Lady's loaf' at the offertory in the eucharist. The image of the Woman clothed with the Sun (Rev. 12.1–6) is also interpreted as having a reference to her.

It should be observed that in some passages of the Scriptures no distinction is drawn between bride and wife (e.g. Rev. 19.7; 22.17).[1] So too the Church applies to Mary as the personal embodiment of the Church such different designations as Mother and Bride. These titles are of course incompatible if interpreted in terms of sex and sexual relations, but in the spiritual realm the incompatibility disappears. The Mother of God as the receptacle of the Holy Spirit bears the Logos within herself, conceives him and gives him birth; she is *Theotokos*. But as a human, created being, as the highest representative of mankind, she is the handmaid of the Lord. As the Church she belongs to the Logos, to Christ, as the Bridegroom and the Head of the Church, and she loves him with the love of the Ever-virgin, *Aeiparthenos*.[2] The Song of Songs is a song about Mary and the Logos as well as about every soul that seeks the heavenly Bridegroom and is united to him. The Virgin Mary, Mother and Bride of God, is the pattern of every soul in its relation to the Logos and to the Church: the soul loves and seeks and finds Christ, is united to him and gives birth to him in itself, and this motherhood and bridal union are indissolubly united; one is impossible without the other. In the Song of Songs the beloved is called by the

---

[1] The *Oxford English Dictionary* defines 'bride': 'A woman about to be married, or very recently married'; 'wife': 'a married woman'. In Rev. 19 and 22 the context is the marriage of the Lamb.

[2] Liddell & Scott define *parthenos* as 'maid, maiden' (*virgo*) or 'girl (not yet married)' (*puella*); *nymphe* as 'bride': 1. a young wife, 2. any married woman, 3. a marriageable maiden.

bridegroom 'my sister, my spouse' (4.9–10), and this does not refer to physical kinship, which is absent (8.1–2). The incarnate Logos becomes a Brother to all mankind, which he has himself taught to call on the heavenly Father in the Lord's Prayer; hence human beings are his brothers and sisters: 'I will declare Thy name unto my brethren: in the midst of the congregation will I praise Thee' (Ps. 22.22; Heb. 2.12); cf. John 20.17: 'go to my brethren, and say unto them'.

Thus is appears that divine motherhood combines love-relations which are mutually incompatible in fallen humanity, which lives a divided and broken, not an integral life. But the designations 'Mother' and 'Bride' refer at the same time to the Church as well as to Mary. The Church is both the Body and Bride of Christ and mother of Christians. This means, at least, that it is animated by Christ and indissolubly united to him, submitting to Him in love and obedience. The Mother of God, having in her no life other than Christ's, is his Body both in a general and in a specific sense. She gives him her own body, bearing him and giving him birth as the fruit of her womb: Christ's union with the Church as his Body is clearly manifested in this. But in virtue of being the Mother of Christ, our Lady is the mother of all mankind which, on the cross, is made hers by adoption in the person of St John; through this, in her and with her, all mankind becomes not only Christ's 'brethren' but also his body.

Further, the Church is the bride or wife of the Logos, and therefore marriage also is made in the likeness of 'Christ and the Church' (Eph. 5.32). A bride and a wife spiritually represent the same relation taken in two different but interconnected aspects: of seeking and finding, striving and attainment, longing and fulfilment. In the corresponding texts of the Scriptures (Eph. 5 and others, and especially the Song of Songs) the relation between Christ and the Church is represented as love and the bliss of love, crowning the longing and seeking. Love is the union of two lives into one common life, a new life; and in this lies the revelation and the bliss of love as well as its torment, experienced when the union is hindered or broken (the beloved seeking her lover in the streets of the city, Song of Songs 3.1–3, 5, 6, 7). In this light, the force and meaning of the Song of Songs and the essential importance which this mysterious hymn of love has for the New Testament conception of the Church become intelligible; indeed, this Song is wholly in the spirit of the New Testament.

Mary as the personal habitation of the Holy Spirit is in truth the true personal expression of the Church, the heart of the Church of which Christ is the Head. Overshadowed by the Holy Spirit, she becomes the Mother of God, brings forth the Logos, and in and through her this divine motherhood belongs to the whole Church; the Logos born of the Virgin is also born in the souls of the faithful, for every Christian soul has a part in the divine motherhood of the Mother-Church, *Theotokos*.[1] The Church and Mary each bear the same relation alike to Christ and Christians. It would be impossible to say in so many words that Mary is the Church, and yet it may be said that the Church is represented by Mary, in so far as in her person all the attributes of the Church find their personal, final, and most perfect embodiment.[2]

The Mother of God has no need of prayer for herself, for as deified she is in possession of all things. As the glory of God and the glory of the world, as the manifested love of God for the world and the manifested love of the world for God, in her prayer she glorifies God. Her own prayer is glorification, eternally realized love, flaming and triumphant in its perfect joy—God's own love for himself in his creation. But as the foremost representative of the world and of all creation, the Mother of God offers also a prayer which is not her own, and yet is hers as the prayer of all creation. She gives wings to its prayer; raising it to the throne of God, she gives it power; she is the intercessor raising her hands to God as a high-priestess (*orante*) and overshadowing the world with her veil. The Mother of God is the praying Church itself in its personal embodiment, and in this sense she is the universal Mother, defender and guardian. She is personal, incarnate mercy and pity for the world in its creaturely shortcomings and sinful distortion. Being now absolutely free from these shortcomings and from the power of sin, she is the sunlit summit of the world, for she still belongs to it. The saints and the prayers of the saints surround this summit like a bright cloud and draw near to it. But even the angelic world and the greatest

[1] St Augustine.   [2] Bulgakov, S. N., op. cit., pp. 188–8.

saints are separated from the Mother of God both by her perfect holiness and by her deification, that is, by the fact that in her creaturely shortcomings are completely overcome: her own gracious life is the life of the Holy Spirit dwelling in her, and her vicarious life is the life of the whole created world to which she belongs. It is in this that her mediatory significance lies: she brings to her Son, the world's Saviour, the world which he has saved; its salvation is realized in and through her, and nothing in the world takes place apart from her. She has given flesh to her Son and she is herself the God-bearing flesh through which the flesh of the world is brought to him for salvation. In her submission to God's will she has spiritually sacrificed her Son's life to God, and as she stood by the cross she was silently continuing to say that which she had said once and forever: 'Behold the handmaid of the Lord.'

We must take the last step in following this line of thought and admit that the outpouring of the Holy Spirit upon all flesh takes place with the participation of the Mother of God, who for that reason was present at Pentecost. The central place she occupies in the Church precludes the possibility of anything in the life of the Church happening apart from her and not through her. Owing to her significance as the habitation of the Holy Spirit, the action of the Holy Spirit in the creature involves her co-operation. This is the explanation of the striking fact that the enormous majority of miraculous and miraculously revealed ikons are ikons of our Lady, and that many of the heavenly visions seen by the saints are visions of her. The churchliness of the Church and the power of entering into it are centred in the Mother of God, and those who have this power come particularly close to her and are 'her kin', as she herself has vouchsafed to say about Saint Seraphim, who was honoured by so many visions of her. And this is why the veneration of our Lady is the measure of churchliness. The Church is the Holy Spirit, the giver of life, and the revelation of the Holy Spirit enables us to understand and to revere the Queen of heaven and earth.[1]

---

[1] Ibid., pp. 203-6.

Jacob's Ladder

The holy angels receive their name not on their own account, as men do, but on account of their calling. Their vocation is to act as intermediaries between God and the world. This is God's will with regard to them; and also, in virtue of their freedom, it is what they choose to be, the expression of angelic love. The power of love lies in its sacrificial character; the essence of it is self-renunciation. The specific nature of angelic love consists in the fact that the angels' personal love (since all love is in the first place personal) for God and the whole of mankind is accompanied by metaphysical self-denial. It involves renouncing their own independent nature and sharing the life of human beings. As incorporeal spirits angels have no part in the natural world. They live by participating in Godhead as derivative lights, and in humanity as guardians of our human nature. In their celestial glory they humble themselves to boundless abasement out of love for God, who wills this service from them, and love for the human world, which could not come into being and live its life without their service. 'Love seeketh not her own' (1 Cor. 13), and angelic love, truly, has not and knows not her own. Incorporeal spirits, pure subsistences, in their free love renounce their selfhood: they live only outside themselves, not their own life; in their metaphysical self-emptying they are in their very nature angels only, personal *metaxu*, mere go-betweens. Such a condition may appear a state of poverty and emptiness, a kind of half-being or pre-existence. And yet in reality it means a superabundance of being, for it manifests the triumphant power of superabundant love. The power and mystery of love consist in dying for resurrection, in life through death, since love is renunciation of self. Created love requires concrete self-renunciation, a sacrifice of one's wealth or possessions, as it is symbolically expressed in the Saviour's words to the rich young man who 'trusted in riches'. Angelic love is metaphysical self-renunciation—not only renunciation of one's 'riches' but of everything of one's own in general. This character of angelic love is negatively expressed by the fall of the spirits who desired something for 'their own' and strove to obtain their kingdom with 'the prince of this world'. But the good angels who 'loved not their lives unto the death' (Rev. 12.11) rejected such striving. In the angelic world this self-denial—willingly undertaken since inspired by love—is a reflection of the divine love. The life of the Holy Trinity is determined by the mutual self-emptying of the divine Persons who find themselves and their life not in themselves but in the Others: the Father in the Son and the Spirit, the Son in the Father and the Spirit, the Spirit in the Father and the Son. In like manner, angels have their life in God and in the human world, reserving for themselves only the 'incorporeal', i.e., natureless, though personal being—only the possibility but not the power of being, reducing themselves as it were to a state of potentiality.

The love of the divine Persons for the world as shown in the creation of it is another aspect of the self-emptying of the Deity which, voluntarily limiting itself, posits beside itself the world's relative being and bestows reality upon it. God gives everything to his creation and takes nothing from it, being all-sufficient, all-blissful, and self-subsistent. The angels' love for our world is similar: it seeks not its own, it merely gives and 'ministers'; it helps man for his own sake to become himself. But the self-renunciation of the angelic love leads to infinite wealth. Through their love for God the holy angels participate in the life of the Deity, and through their love for the world they participate in the life of our world and live it while transcending it by nature. Thus they combine in themselves the utmost fullness of life accessible to created beings: life in God and life in the human world. The world's all is given to the angels at their creation, but they acquire that all through their ministration. The life of angels who are created spirits differs from the divine life, in which it is given them to participate. It differs too from the life of the human world, but has a share in it in virtue of the angels' service. But first and foremost their life is personal love which finds for itself a Friend and friends in God and man. For the Lord, too, in giving everything to his creation and taking nothing from it, wants from it one thing only, love, and seeks to find in angels and in men his 'other', a friend.

The world is overshadowed by angels' wings. The eyes of the angels watch unceasingly over us. Holy angels continually ascend and descend between the heavens and the earth. They unite themselves to us in our prayers. Heavenly hosts continually glorify the Creator. The angels who stand before the throne of God live a life in common with us, united to us by bonds of love. How great is the joy given to man in the knowledge of this![1]

'Praise him, all ye angels of his: praise him, all His host!'[2]
'Holy angels and archangels, pray to God for us!'
'Holy guardian-angel, pray to God for us!'

[1] Bulgakov, S. N., *Lestvitsa Iakovlya* (Paris, 1929), pp. 227–9.
[2] Ps. 148.2.

By Jacob's Well

An article on the actual unity of the apparently
divided Church: in prayer, faith, and sacrament.

John 4.23

The language of the New Testament frequently contains the
term 'the Church' or 'the Churches'. On the one hand there
is the mystical unity of the Church as the Body of Christ; on
the other hand there are the specific communities in which
such life was realized. We still use the same terms, not only
in the above-mentioned sense but also in that of different
Christian confessions. We must admit that such a use of the
word 'Churches' often shocks us, for in our own minds, for
example, we often think that actually there exists only one
Church, namely the Orthodox Church; whereas all that
stands outside Orthodoxy is not the Church. But the evidence
of the use of language cannot be explained away by mere
civility or hypocrisy, for it contains a concept that a sort of
these 'non-Churches' belongs to 'the Church'. For actually
these Churches are distinct to us from the non-Christian world.
Already in the gospel narrative we trace this relativeness in
connection with the idea of the Church. Our Lord, who came
not to destroy the law but to fulfil it, belonged himself to the
Jewish Church. He was a faithful Israelite carrying out its
precepts, and this in spite of all its exclusiveness. And yet we
get a solemn witness about the Church Universal in our Lord's
conversation with the Samaritan woman by Jacob's Well.
We are equally struck here both by the very fact that this
conversation (which so astonished the disciples) took place,
and by the universal 'good news' of Our Lord's message:
'Believe Me, the hour cometh when neither in this mountain
nor in Jerusalem, shall ye worship the Father . . . the hour
cometh and now is, when the true worshippers shall worship
the Father in spirit and in truth: for such doth the Father seek
to be His worshippers.'[1] And he then reveals to her, a Samaritan, that he is the Christ.

[1] John 4.21, 23.

All the events in the life of our Lord have not only a temporary but also an eternal significance, and this is also true of this conversation with the Samaritan woman. For even at the present time we find that we stand by Jacob's Well and also ask Jesus Christ about where and how we must worship the Lord. And even now we, who are the 'Jews', know what we worship 'for salvation is from the Jews' (*'nulla salus extra ecclasiam'*). And in our day also our Lord reveals himself to the Samaritan woman and calls on all to worship in spirit and in truth. The harsh, unbending, unrelenting institutionalism of the one saving Church conflicts here with a service in the Spirit, which 'bloweth where it listeth, and thou hearest the voice thereof, but knowest not whence it cometh, and whither it goeth'.[1] There exists between the Church and the Churches not only a relationship of mutual expulsion but also one of concordance. This unity is simultaneously something already given and something we must attain to. No single historical Church can so confine its attention to itself alone as to ignore the Christian world beyond its own limits. Even heresies and schisms are manifestations taking place only within the life of the Church—for pagans and men of other faiths are not heretics and schismatics to us. One can picture differently the ways to Church unity, but its very existence already assumes the fact of actual unity. The Church is one, as life in Christ by the Holy Spirit is one. Only, participation in this unity can be of varying degrees and depths.

Therefore, quite naturally, there are two aspects in the relation of Orthodoxy to non-Orthodoxy: a repulsion in the struggle of truth with an incomplete truth, and a mutual attraction of Church love. History and a sad realism apprehend more of the former aspect of this relationship, for the spirit of schism and division is not only a characteristic of 'heretics' and 'schismatics'. The will for division is the evil genius which first split up the West and the East, and which ever since pursues its devastating work further and further.

But can the realization of the truth of our Church be silenced even for a moment, or conversely, can we ever fail to be aware of the untruth of those who think differently? Might not such an attitude result in the sin of lack of faith,

[1] John 3.8.

which seeks to avoid confessing its own truth and perhaps suffering for it? And so in repulsion and attraction, unity and division, we see a peculiar dialectic of Church life, which comprises the thesis and the antithesis, and we observe that the greater the exertion of the one, the acuter the other. The way of 'ecumenical' Church life, which strived for Church unity, is simultaneously associated both with a fuller realization of confessional differences and a growing consciousness of unity. But although there seems to be no escape from this antinomy, the Spirit of God actually transcends it through a new kind of synthesis that is brought about, not by means of a new agreement or compromise, but by a new inspiration. The distinction between various confessions lies first of all in dogmatic differences, and then in the religious and practical discrepancies which result from them. These are on the surface and are apparent to all. But that which constitutes Church unity, that which is already given, and the striving towards unity, which actually exists as the basis of unity—this is hidden in the very depths. Meanwhile this task is a duty both of Church love and of practical utility. One must realize and express the positive spiritual basis of Christian 'ecumenism' not only as an idea but as an actuality existing by grace. We experience it as a breathing of God's Spirit in grace, as a revelation of Pentecost, when people begin to understand one another in spite of the diversity of tongues.

Let us try to express quite concisely this positive basis of unity, which actually exists even now in the Christian world.

1 PRAYER

The division which occurred in the Church, whatever its origin, was associated with a separation in prayer and remains as an unhealed wound in the Body of the Church. Such is the logic of our frail nature, which cannot contain the entire truth, but only parts of it. Dissociation in prayer, having once arisen, strives to become permanent, lasting, and constant. We are now faced by the strange and provoking sight of Christians praying to God and their Saviour, our Lord Jesus Christ, in separate communities. Moreover this division is enforced in the rules of the Church, which arose, it is true, in the fourth and fifth centuries, but which retain even now the force of actual law. They have not been cancelled formally, although life itself cancels them. The general purpose of these rules in the first place was of course to banish 'indifference' by applying protective measures, which were then in accord with the acute struggle with heresy. But measures of defence lose their significance when there is no attacking party—and we see this state of affairs in a whole range of interconfessional relationships in our own time. We are bound to recognize not only that which separates us, but also that which remains common to us all, notwithstanding all divisions. The ability to distinguish in life all that constitutes the common heritage of the whole Christian world is the great achievement (only possible through grace) of contemporary 'ecumenism', namely the movement striving for Church unity. An encounter between Christians of different confessions, as Christians, is a great joy which is bestowed on us in our time by the Holy Spirit and a new revelation of the universal Pentecost. Nothing is easier to criticize than this 'pan-Christianity' by pointing out that there can exist no 'Christianity in general' but only one true Church in its indestructible concreteness and wholeness. This is true, no doubt, in the sense that the fullness of worship in an ordained and divinely inspired cult can only exist in unanimity. But even so there still remains Christianity as such, as faith in our Lord, love for him, and worship directed to him, and this Christianity endures not only in Orthodoxy but as something common to all confessions. We are particularly clear about this and aware of it in missionary work where Christians are compelled, when confronted by pagans, to get a fuller and deeper consciousness of their own Christianity.

The united prayer of Christians, belonging to different confessions, in Churches and outside them, is becoming a more and more usual occurrence at the present time. This new practice is not merely a liberty which is quite out of place where strict discipline is exercised, but a common Christian achievement, a capacity for uniting in that which is an actual reality. A time will dawn when the Orthodox Church will define certain rules for this practice and will give the required directions. Meanwhile all this is done in a groping manner, as circumstances demand. This united common prayer can be based dogmatically on the fact that the Name of our Lord is hallowed and called on by all Christians. Christ is present in his Name to each one who prays thus, 'for where two or three are gathered together in My Name, there am I in the midst of them'.[1] In truth all Christians who call on Christ's Name in prayer are already actually one with Christ; when we lift our eyes to heaven, earthly barriers cease to exist for us.

But is this actually so? Do these barriers remain even in our union in prayer? Yes, in a certain sense they remain. For we cannot unite in everything with our brethren in prayer. For example, we cannot pray together to the blessed Virgin and to the saints with Protestants. We can find differences in worship even with Roman Catholics, although these differences may not be so essential. But we are not compelled to be silent about these differences, and, if so, is this not treason to Orthodoxy? We must not close our eyes to the fact that such dangers, generally speaking, do exist. The position of Orthodoxy in its relation to the Protestant world is especially unfavourable in this case, precisely because Orthodoxy for the sake of communion in prayer is forced to adapt itself by, as it were, minimizing itself, thereby losing some of its fullness. Of course, if this is done out of love for the sake of Church 'economy' it is permissible, for it is then regarded as a sacrifice of love, in accordance with the Apostle Paul's principle of being 'all things to all men'. Our brethren, however, should realize that this is only a sacrifice of love and a condescension to their weakness, not a denial of our own faith.

However, in communion in worship with the non-Orthodox we must 'know our measure' so that no distortions or poverty may result in our prayer life. But there is also a positive side to this communion in prayer. We are wont to pride ourselves on our liturgical wealth, as compared to the severe and simple rites of the Protestants. And yet we must not close our eyes to the fact that in actual practice we are far from realizing to the full this wealth of ours, so that in some instances it lies upon us as a dead weight of custom. Protestantism, in spite of its apparent liturgical poverty, knows a living extempore prayer, in which the human soul in a childlike way turns directly to our Father in heaven. This is the wealth of Protestantism even though it is associated with liturgical poverty.

[1] Matt. 18.20.

2 THE WORD OF GOD

The holy Gospels are the common property of the entire Christian world. Through the Gospels Christ himself speaks directly to the human soul. The soul listens to him and adores him in worship. Generally in our attitude to the non-Orthodox we underestimate the power of the Gospels. The four Gospels give us a marvellous ikon of our Saviour, drawn by the Holy Spirit of God—a veritable ikon in words. When the Eternal Book is studied not only by the mind but also with the heart, when the soul 'bows down over the Gospels', then the sacrament of the Word, born in that soul, is celebrated.

People incline to minimize this direct impact of the Word of God (*efficacitas verbi*) addressed to every single soul, stressing in an exaggerated way the significance of Holy Tradition for its correct understanding. In practice the significance of Holy Tradition for a living response to the Word of God should not be exaggerated. It has bearing on theology and on certain disputed questions of a dogmatic nature. One might add here that the importance of tradition does not in any way exclude but actually presupposes a direct response to the Word of God, which has its life in the Church—both in its *soborny* consciousness (tradition) and in personal interpretation. And what is especially important is the fact that nothing can replace our personal life with the Gospel (the same applies to the whole Bible). We should be ready to admit the fact that among Orthodox nations the personal reading of the Word of God is considerably less widespread than it is among Protestants, though this is partly replaced by its use in divine worship. The Bible and the Gospels are common Christian property, and the entire Christian world without distinction of confession bends in prayer over the Gospels. It may be urged that a true understanding of the Gospels is only given to the Church. This is, of course, the case in one sense, yet sincere and devout readers of the Gospels through this alone are already within the Church, that is, in the one and Evangelical Church.

3 THE SPIRITUAL LIFE

A Christian who lives in the Church necessarily has also his personal life in Christ, which is simultaneously both personal and 'of the Church'. Dogma and dogmatic peculiarities cannot fail to be reflected in this personal experience. But in the absence of Christological differences there is a very wide field of common faith, even where dogmatic divergences actually do exist. For can one say that 'Christ is divided' for a contemporary Orthodox, Roman Catholic, or believing Protestant? In their love of our Lord and their striving towards him all Christians are one. This is why the language of the mystics and their experience is common to all. We find that spiritual life, in which the divine is really tasted, unites Christians to a far greater extent than does dogmatic perception. When we sense these tremulous contacts our souls respond to them independently of confessional relationships. It may be that this is the most important result of inter-relations of various confessions, which though not reflected in formulae and resolutions represent a spiritual reality. During the Lausanne Conference this feeling of a kind of common spiritual experience of unity in Christ was remarkably strong. It became clear to all that something had happened above and beyond anything written down in the reports and minutes. On the other hand, apart from this kind of experience as such, there cannot be any Christian unity; for this can only be realized through Christian inspiration in a new vision of Pentecost, for which we aspire and which, in part, we already obtain. This unity in Christ, established by the similarity of Christian experience, is a kind of spiritual communion of all in the one Christ, established long before Communion from the same chalice can take place. This *de facto* similarity in the experience of the Christian world, in spite of all its multiplicity, is insufficiently realized. Unfortunately we tend to stress our dogmatic disagreements much more than our common Christian heritage. A mystical intercommunion has always existed among Christians, and in our days more so than previously. Mutual fellowship among the representatives of theological thought, an interchange of ideas, scientific and theological research, a kind of life in common 'over the gospel' —all this tends to make the existing division between Christian confessions already to a certain extent unreal. Symbolic theology is also tending more and more to become 'comparative' instead of being 'denunciatory'. This is even more evident when we come to mystical, pastoral, and ascetic works, and especially to the lives of the saints. With what attention and devotion the Western world (for example Anglicanism) gazes at the images of the Russian saints, or conversely, with what interest we ourselves regard the images of the Western saints, such as St Genevieve, St Francis of Assisi, and others. And we ought to cultivate deliberately this spiritual interpenetration which is naturally increasing more and more. In this way we shall appropriate to ourselves the gifts which have been bestowed on others, and through comparison we shall come to know our own nature more fully and deeply.

Thus there exists even now a certain spiritual unity within the Christian world, although this is not expressed in any formulae. But we should add to this mystical, adogmatic unity of the Christian world the reality of its dogmatic oneness. Owing to certain onesidedness, Christians of various confessions are acutely sensitive to their dogmatic differences, while they do not feel their mutual agreement in the same way. The definition 'heretic', which is really only applicable to certain features of a world outlook, is extended to the entire man, who is completely anathematized for a particular heresy. This was so throughout the course of Christian history. But it would be absolutely inconsistent for us to adopt such language today. For it is time at last to say openly that there exist no heretics in the general sense of the term, but only in a special and particular sense. Such an interpretation, among many others, can be given to the words of the Apostle Paul: 'For there must be also heresies among you.'[1] Of course, in itself, a special heresy stands also for a common affliction, which is detrimental to the spiritual life without, however, destroying it. And it is perhaps difficult and impossible for us really to define the extent of this damage during the epoch when the particular dogmatic division arose. We must not also lose sight of the fact that in addition to heresies of the mind there exist heresies of life, or onesidedness. One can, while remaining an Orthodox, actually tend towards monophysitism in practice, by leaning either towards docetic spiritualism or Manicheism, or towards Nestorianism by separating the two natures in Christ, which leads in practice to the 'secularization' of

[1] 1 Cor. 11.18–19.

culture. And perhaps in this sense it will be found that we all are heretics in various ways. Yet it by no means follows from this that Orthodoxy and the Orthodox do not exist. It only shows that heresy, as such, impairs though it does not destroy life in Christ and in his Church. The notion of a heresy, as of a division, only exists within the limits of the Church and not outside it, and it implies a defectiveness in Church life. It is therefore a mistake to interpret dogmatic anathematizing as a spiritual death-warrant or a complete severing from the Church. As a measure of discipline an anathema is a spiritual death-warrant for a particular Church community, for it represents a separation from the fellowship of the Church. But this disciplinary measure cannot and must not be extended to the whole life of the Church, for even the heretics remain in the Church, and it is not given to us to know to what degree they are condemned because of their heresy.

From this it follows that if heresy is only partial damage we must take into account in dealing with heretics not only that which is heretical but also that which is Orthodox in them. For example, through having an incorrect doctrine on the Filioque, do Roman Catholics cease to believe in the redemptive work of our Lord, or in the sacraments of the Church? And although this seems obvious, yet all Christians must realize not only their divisions but also their agreement. Our Creed, the Nicene Creed (it is true, in its defective form owing to the Filioque), together with the ancient Apostolic and Athanasian Creeds, constitute the general confession of Orthodoxy, Roman Catholicism, and Protestantism, and we must never lose sight of this basis of our dogmatic unity.

3 THE SACRAMENTS

At the present time it is in the sacraments that the Christian confessions are most effectively separated from one another. Sacramental fellowship is still only a remote aim, which still remains unaccomplished in the relationships between Orthodoxy, Roman Catholicism, and Protestantism. In the relation between Orthodoxy and Roman Catholicism on the one hand, and Protestantism on the other, the main barrier is the absence of valid orders and apostolic succession. This barrier does not arise between the first two confessions. Now in the vast majority of Christian confessions sacraments are recognized, in spite of all the diversity of theological teaching associated with them. What attitude ought we to adopt towards the efficacy of these sacraments, and in what measure can this or that theological interpretation associated with them be considered decisive? Although the latter can effect the efficacy of sacraments (only, however, from the side of *ex opere operantis*, and not of *ex opere operato*), nevertheless, given the existence of a common faith, say in the Eucharist, the significance of doctrinal diversity in the realm of eucharistic theology may be greatly exaggerated.

We ought to insist first of all, as a general principle, on the efficacy of the sacraments in various Church communities. But can we adopt such a principle as our guiding line? Or are sacraments, generally speaking, ineffective beyond the canonical limits of a Church organization, to be regarded only as devout customs, or according to the blasphemous opinion of some as 'sacraments of the demons'? The last opinion is the child of confessional fanaticism which can never be confirmed by theological arguments, and is on the contrary in direct contradiction to the true mind of the Church. One might also add that a mere recognition of the power of the sacraments outside Orthodoxy is sufficient, for such a reduction of the question merely to that of their subjective effectiveness (*ex opere operantis*) evades a direct answer to the question as to their objective value (*ex opere operato*). It undoubtedly holds that, in the absence of canonical Church fellowship, the sacraments celebrated outside the canonical limits of a given Church organization canonically and practically, as it were, cease to exist. But does this canonical ineffectiveness (*nonefficacitas*) imply their mystical invalidity (*nonvaliditas*)? Does it mean that on being separated canonically and in a certain measure dogmatically also, we find that we are separated from our mysterious unity and fellowship in Christ and in the gifts of the Holy Spirit? Has Christ been really divided in us, or are the non-Orthodox thereby no longer 'in Christ', being estranged from his Body? One ought to think deeply before answering this question, which is perhaps the most essential for us in our relations with the non-Orthodox. It falls into two questions: the significance of canonical divisions and that of dogmatic divisions, in relation to effectiveness of sacraments.

The first question is answered by stating that canonical divisions (*raskol*) only prevent the possibility of a direct and unmediated communion in the sacraments and do not destroy their efficacy. The invisible fellowship therefore of those who have been separated is not broken. This constitutes great joy and consolation when we are faced with the sad and sinful fact of canonical divisions in the Church. We ought to consider that although we are canonically divided from the Roman Catholic Church, we never ceased to remain with it in an invisible sacramental communion (*ex opere operato*, so to speak). Generally speaking, if one wanted to be consistent in denying the efficacy of the sacraments on a canonical basis one could only do it by accepting the Roman Catholic teaching on the supremacy of the Pope and obedience to his jurisdiction as an essential condition of belonging to the Church. However such a deduction is not made even by the Roman Catholic Church, which admits the effectiveness of sacraments in Orthodoxy. The Romanizing tendency in Orthodoxy sometimes goes further than Rome in this direction, conditioning the effectiveness of the sacrament by canonical stipulations, though theologically such a point of view cannot be supported. Conversely one could say that the divided parts of the Church, at least where apostolic succession exists, are in an invisible, mysterious communion with one another through visible sacraments, although these are mutually inaccessible.

Now let us consider to what extent a digression from dogmatic teaching can destroy the efficacy of the sacrament. We ought to mention here, first of all, the cases where the damage affects not separate sacraments but their celebrants. We speak here of Protestantism, where, through the destruction of a rightly ordained priesthood through grace, the question of the actual efficacy of the sacrament is raised in spite of its full recognition in principle. Can one speak of 'sacraments' in Protestantism? Fortunately there are grounds for answering this question not only in the negative. The basis of the answer lies in the fact that the Church recognizes the efficacy of Protestant baptism, which is evident from the fact that it does not re-baptize Protestants who join it. This admission is of extraordinary significance. It testifies to the fact that at least as regards the sacrament of spiritual birth in the Church we abide in fellowship with Protestants as Christians and members of the one Body of Christ. Baptism also contains within itself the general possibility of a mysterious life in the Church; in this sense it is the potential of all future sacraments. In Protestantism they only have a partial existence, both because of the diminution of the number of sacraments and especially through the absence of priesthood. But even so, does this allow us to draw any conclusion as to the complete inefficacy of sacramental life in Protestantism, in particular, for example, as regards Holy Communion? Strictly speaking we have no right to come to such a conclusion, and not only because of the subjective basis pointed out by Bishop Theophanes, but also because of the objective principle of a sacrament according to which the sacrament belongs to the entire Church, although it is realized through the priesthood by virtue of its inevitable participation. There is no such priesthood in Protestantism, but the people of the Church, the 'royal priesthood', remains there, and the potential power of Holy Baptism is fulfilled and revealed there in other ways, in certain devout rites and prayers instead of in effective sacraments. But if these are ineffective, can we say that they are nothing? One cannot say this, for the priesthood is not a magical apparatus for the celebration of sacraments but a ministration of the Church which exists in the Church and for the Church. Therefore we ought to interpret Theophanes' expression 'according to their faith it shall be given them' in the sense that our Lord does not deprive this flock of his grace, although it has been separated from the fullness of Church life. Nevertheless we can speak of communion in sacraments (apart from baptism) in relation to Protestants only in the general and indefinite sense of their participation in the life of the Church through grace, but of nothing beyond this. A more direct and true communion in sacraments with the Protestant world is hindered by the absence of a rightly ordained priesthood: this is the threshold over which Protestantism must pass, the re-establishment of an apostolically ordained hierarchy.

These barriers do not exist, however, for those sections of

the divided Church which have retained this succession and have therefore a correctly ordained priesthood. Orthodoxy and Roman Catholicism belong to this category, together with the ancient Eastern Churches (as well as the Episcopal Church in Protestantism and Anglicanism, in particular in the case of a positive solution of the question of Anglican ordination). The priesthood of Roman Catholicism and Orthodoxy are mutually uncanonical owing to the existing schism, but this does not prevent their mutually recognizing each other. The following conclusion of the utmost importance follows from this: Churches which have preserved their priesthood, although they happen to be separated, are not actually divided in their sacramental life. Strictly speaking a reunion of the Church is not even necessary here, although generally this is hardly realized. The Churches which have preserved such a unity in sacraments are now divided canonically in the sense of jurisdiction, and dogmatically, through a whole range of differences; but these are powerless to destroy the efficacy of the sacraments.

What is required for a complete reunion, and where do we start? The predominant formula runs: sacramental fellowship must be preceded by a preliminary dogmatic agreement. But is this axiom so indisputable as it appears? Here on one scale of the balance we have a difference in certain Christian dogmas and theological opinions, and an estrangement which has been formed through centuries; on the other we have the unity of sacramental life. May it not be that a unity in the sacrament will be the only way towards overcoming this difference? Why should we not seek to surmount a heresy in teaching through superseding a heresy of life such as division? May it not be that Christians sin now by not heeding the common eucharistic call? And, if this is so, then for Orthodoxy and Rome there still remains a way to their reunion on the basis of a fellowship in sacraments.

Of course, the Holy Spirit alone can make it clear that reunion is not far away but already exists as a fact which only needs to be realized. But it must be realized sincerely and honestly for the sole purpose of expressing our brotherhood in the Lord. And the way towards the reunion of East and West does not lie through tournaments between the theologians of the East and West, but through a reunion before the Altar. The priesthood of the East and the West must realize itself as one priesthood, celebrating the one Eucharist, and, if the minds of the priests could become aflame with this idea, all barriers would fall. For in response to this, dogmatic unity will be achieved, or rather a mutual understanding of one another in our distinctive features. '*In necessariis unitas, in dubiis libertas, in omnibus charitas.*'

A realization of our unity as something given and at the same time of our disunity as a fact which we cannot ignore is present as a vital antithesis in the soul of the modern Christian. This antinomy cannot leave him in peace. He cannot remain indifferent to it, for he must seek its resolution. The Ecumenical Movement of today is the expression of this search.[1]

---

[1] Bulgakov, S. N., 'By Jacob's Well', in *Journal of the Fellowship of St Alban and St Sergius* (London, 1933), No. 22.

The Lamb of God

And the Spirit and the bride say, come.
And let him who heareth say, come.
Rev. 22.17

The salvation wrought by Christ takes place in the individual soul which is more precious than the world, and the path to it is struggle with sin, tragic laceration in the soul of fallen man, subjection of the flesh to the spirit, and acceptance of the cross of Christ. This truth has always stood in the centre of Christian life and is clearly understood and undisputed. There is, however, no such clear understanding of the other aspect of the truth about salvation as not merely personal but universal, inclusive of the whole Church—as Christ's kingdom in the world.

The kings of the earth and the rulers long ago set themselves against the Lord and again his Anointed. Indeed they did so at the very beginning of Church history; they rebelled not openly but by sly subterfuges tried to belittle, to limit, to falsify, to render void God's coming in the flesh, to nullify God-manhood and to keep the world in the hands of its prince. Docetism and Gnosticism, Manicheanism and transcendentalism, Hinduism and Jesuitism—innumerable conscious and semi-conscious opponents of God-manhood, under the pretext of gnosis, piety, asceticism, moralism, and spirituality, deny the power of the Incarnation and seek to disincarnate the Logos. This is also the burden of the envious, antitheistic, and anti-Christian anthropocentrism which puts man in the place of the God-man, the incarnate Word.

The motley army of Antichrist has succeeded in bullying mankind into the belief that Christ has gone from the world and forsaken it and that his kingdom, which is not of this world, shall never in any way be attained on earth. Accordingly, aims must be lowered, symbols must be taken as final achievements, and we must either be resigned to incompleteness and inevitable inadequacy or simply escape—

actually or spiritually, ascetically or theologically, into the desert of negation, indifference, and pride, since this world, reserved unto fire, exists merely in order to be ascetically rejected. And, like a snake gliding along the ground, a whispered question spreads far and wide: to whom then does the world belong? To the God-man or to the man-god? To Christ or to Antichrist?

Can it be true that Christ came to save the world and that the prince of this world is banished, and 'the last time' is a time of his last convulsions when he rages, knowing that his end has come? In answer to the blasphemous question of half-belief the enemies of God rise up in rebellion against the Holy. The beast and the false prophet, Gog and Magog, besiege the camp of the saints and through fear and deception make men receive the mark of the beast, without which 'no man might buy or sell' or indeed have any place on earth. The whole power of evil, heresy, and unbelief is now centred round this lie: the world is not Christ's but its own! And those in whom the dominant lie has not altogether destroyed faith in Christ's coming in glory and power are troubled by the sore question: who shall roll us away the stone from the door of the sepulchre, for it is very great? But 'all things are possible to him that believeth', and by faith we know that God-manhood is the divine miracle in the world and that the stone shall be rolled away by an angel through the power of Christ.

The seer who was shown things which must shortly come to pass saw that in heaven in the midst of the throne stood the Lamb as if it had been slain, having seven horns, and he was worshipped because he is 'worthy to receive power, and riches, and wisdom, and strength, and honour, and glory, and blessing', and the kingdom of this world became the kingdom of Christ, the Lord of lords, 'kings and high priests'. A new feeling for life is being born in Christians—the feeling that man must not run away from the world, for Christ is coming into the world to the marriage feast of the Lamb, the feast of deified humanity, coming as a King and therefore as a Judge. In their struggle for the kingdom of Christ the faithful turn to the coming Christ; hearts are lifted up in expectation of him, and the forgotten prayer of the first Christians begins,

though as yet timidly, to be heard again: 'Even so, come!'
In their heresy about the world and disbelief in Christ as its
King, Christians have unlearned this prayer; it has been
encompassed by fear, which is, however, overcome by love.
But it still remains the Easter hymn of Christian mankind,
for Christ is the King who comes in the name of the Lord.

Christ's exhaustion on the cross shows how his divine nature
humbles itself to fit human measure. His divinity is self-
constrained to yield to death, and though it does not itself
die, it bears the weight of his dying humanity. It is his divine
hypostasis itself that thus shares in death, for it is the hypostasis of his human nature indissolubly united with the
divine. Therefore it is the God-man in the integral unity of his
complex being who dies, but dies differently in his respective
natures: the human nature dies, and consequently its hypostasis, which is the divine hypostasis of the Logos, passes with
it through the gates of death to the depths of creaturely non-
being. It thus brings to the utmost diminution in death its
divine nature as well. In this sense death extends to the whole
God-man, both to his humanity and to his divinity, though
in a different way, and therefore it is quite impossible to
exclude his divinity from participation in death.

The same idea must be carried further and applied not only
to the Logos himself, but to the other Persons of the Holy
Trinity. Here we could think about the last two cries from the
cross. The first is the God-forsakenness, indicating a kind of
sinking of the Son out of sight of the Father, his link with
whom is thus known only in the pain of yearning. Now the
Son calls to him out of the depths of the creatureliness of his
human nature. This forsaking the Son is an act of the Father,
expressing his acceptance of the Son's death, and to that
extent the Father's participation in it. To leave the Son to
die on the Cross is for the Father a spiritual participation in
the vicarious sacrifice of love, though the Father did not die.
No less significant of this participation of the Father in the
Son's exhaustion on the cross is the Son's last cry, committing
his spirit unto the hands of the Father. The Son returns to the
Father's bosom, though not as yet to abide there beyond all
worlds and to sit on the right hand of the Father as in the
glorious Ascension. The incarnate Son is as it were forcibly

made discarnate in death, and his divine-human spirit returns to his Father and his God, just as in human death the dust returns to the earth and the spirit 'unto God Who gave it'.[1] This is a special depth of abasement in the self-humbling of the Son, in which the Father takes part in his own way. It is the Father who accepts the spirit of the Son and shelters it for the three days before the resurrection. The spirits of all whom God sends to the earth return to him in death, and it is, so to speak, as one of these spirits that the Father receives the spirit of the Son who has tasted death. The Son's commitment into the Father's hands signifies the deepest self-lowering of divinity. A divine mystery, inaccessible to human understanding, is hidden in the Father's acceptance of the Son in the exhaustion of death and his tending of him until the resurrection; but we touch reverently upon this mystery, since the holy gospel bears witness to it.

The Son's God-forsakenness and the exhaustion of his divinity implies that the Holy Spirit, while ever resting upon the God-man, yet somehow forsakes him also. For the Holy Spirit is, first and foremost, the perceptible nearness of the Father, abiding in his love. The Holy Spirit is the actual personal love of the Father for the Son and of the Son for the Father, their unity, itself hypostatic (this is why Christ's words 'I and the Father are one' tacitly assume 'in the Holy Spirit'). The state of God-forsakenness as sinking out of sight of the Father necessarily implies being also forsaken by the Holy Spirit, who descended upon the Son when he was plunged in the waters of Jordan, which symbolized his coming death. The Holy Spirit returned, as it were, once more to the Father when death had taken place in complete God-forsakenness (and indeed apart from this God-forsakenness death could not have taken place in the God-man). Since, then, the Holy Spirit acquiesces in this way in the self-emptying of the Son, in his exhaustion on the cross, he also spends himself with him; for to refrain from manifesting oneself to the beloved is to do violence to love, *a fortiori* for him whose being is love. (The human image of this self-shedding of the Spirit is given by the Mother of God standing by the cross while a sword was piercing through her soul, and her Son entrusting her to the care

[1] Eccl. 12.7.

of the beloved disciple.) The Holy Spirit is joy, he is the comforter, but the Son in his agony on the cross was left without joy and comfort; he found comfort only in obedience to the will of the Father and in prayer.[1]

In coming down from heaven, in his nativity, the Son leaves the heavenly glory of the Holy Trinity; in going down into the bowels of the earth the Son as it were surrenders his place as God in God, and his divine hypostasis ('My Spirit') is committed to the Father's care.[2]

---

[1] Heb. 5.7.
[2] Bulgakov, S. N., *Agnets Bozhii* (Paris, 1933), pp. 343 ff.

The Orthodox Church

Orthodoxy is the Church of Christ on earth. The Church of Christ is not an institution; it is a new life with Christ and in Christ, guided by the Holy Spirit. Christ, the Son of God, came to earth, was made man, uniting his divine life with that of humanity. This divine-human life he gave to his brethren, who believe on his name. Although he died and rose again and ascended into heaven, he was not separated from his humanity but remains in it. The light of the resurrection of Christ lights the Church, and the joy of resurrection, of the triumph over death, fills it. The risen Lord lives with us, and our life in the Church is a mysterious life in Christ. 'Christians' bear that name precisely because they belong to Christ. They live in Christ and Christ lives in them. The Incarnation is not only an idea or a doctrine; it is above all an event which happened once in time but which possesses all the power of eternity, and this perpetual incarnation, a perfect, indissoluble union, yet without confusion, of the two natures, divine and human, makes the Church. Since the Lord did not merely approach humanity but became one with it, himself becoming man, the Church is the Body of Christ, as a unity of life with him, a life subordinate to him and under his authority. The same idea is expressed when the Church is called the Bride of Christ or of the Word. The relations between bride and bridegroom, taken in their everlasting fullness, consist of a perfect unity of life, a unity which preserves the reality of their difference; it is a union of two in one, which is not dissolved by duality nor absorbed by unity.

The Church, although it is the Body of Christ, is not the Christ—the God-Man—because it is only his humanity; but it is life in Christ, and with Christ, the life of Christ in us: 'It is no longer I who live, but Christ who liveth in me.'[1] But Christ is not only a divine Person. Since his own life is

[1] Gal. 2.20.

inseparable from that of the Holy Trinity,[1] his life is consubstantial with that of the Father and the Holy Spirit. Thus it is that, although a life in Christ, the Church is also a life in the Holy Trinity. The Body of Christ lives in Christ, and by that very fact in the Holy Trinity. Christ is the Son. In him we learn to know the Father; we are adopted by God, to whom we cry, 'Our Father'.

The love of God, the love of the Father for the Son and that of the Son for the Father, is not a simple quality or relation; it possesses itself a personal life. It is hypostatic. The love of God is the Holy Spirit, which proceeds from the Father to the Son, abiding upon him. The Son exists for the Father only in the Holy Spirit which rests on him, as the Father manifests his love for the Son by the Holy Spirit, which is the unity of life of Father and Son. And the Spirit himself, being the love of two persons, in keeping with the very nature of love, lives, so to speak, in his personal existence outside himself in the Father and the Son. This is love: living, it dies, and dying, it lives. In the moment when it seems to efface itself, it exercises the greatest force. This is the place of the Holy Spirit in the Holy Trinity.

The Church, in her quality of Body of Christ, which lives with the life of Christ, is by that fact the domain where the Holy Spirit lives and works. More than this, the Church is life by the Holy Spirit, because it is the Body of Christ. This is why the Church may be considered as a blessed life in the Holy Spirit, or the life of the Holy Spirit in humanity.[2]

The fullness of the true faith, the true doctrine, is much too vast to be held in the consciousness of an isolated member of the Church. Tradition is the living memory of the Church, containing the true doctrine that manifests itself in its history. It is not an archaeological museum, not a scientific catalogue; it is not, furthermore, a dead depository. No! tradition is a living power inherent in a living organism. In the stream of

---

[1] '*Il est "l'une des personnes" de la Sainte Trinité*' (French edn, Paris, 1932). [Ed.]

[2] Bulgakov, S. N., *The Orthodox Church* (London, 1935), pp. 9 ff. Though the present text has been revised, references are to the English text of 1935. A French edition appeared in 1932 and a Romanian translation in 1933. [Ed.]

its life it bears along the past in all its forms so that all the past is contained in the present and is the present. The unity and continuity of tradition follow from the fact that the Church is always identical with itself. The Church has a unique life, guided at all times by the Holy Spirit; the historical form changes, but the spirit remains unchanged. Thus belief in Church tradition as the basic source of Church doctrine arises from a belief in the unity and self-identity of the Church. The period of primitive Christianity is very unlike the present time, yet one must admit that it is the same Church like unto itself; by its unity of life, the Church binds together the communities of Paul and the local churches of today.

In different epochs, it is true, tradition has not been known and comprehended in the same degree by all members of the Church, and it may be said that in actual fact tradition is inexhaustible, for it is the very life of the Church. But it remains living and active, even when it continues unknown. The essential principle of tradition is this: each member of the Church, in his life and his knowledge (whether it concerns scientific theology or practical wisdom) should seek to attain the integral unity of tradition, to test himself if he is in accord with it. He ought to carry in himself living tradition; he ought to be a link inseparably connected with all the chain of history.[1]

The tradition of the Church is an exterior, phenomenal manifestation of the inner, noumenal unity of the Church. It must be comprehended as a living force, as the consciousness of a single organism, in which all its previous life is included. Thus tradition is uninterrupted and inexhaustible; it is not only the past but also the present, in which the future lives as well. We have an image of living tradition in the relationship between Old and New Testaments. The Old Testament is not abrogated but completed by the New. Still the Old contains the New within itself in a preparatory form, as its own fulfilment, its own future. And from the Old Testament there stream rays of light into the new age, beyond the Second Coming—light which extends from the Creator to the fulfilment, when he shall be 'all in all'.

[1] Ibid., pp. 19 ff.

Tradition is not a sort of archaeology, which by its shadows connects the present with the past, nor a law, it is the fact that the life of the Church remains always identical with itself. Tradition receives a 'normative' value precisely because of this identity. And as the same spirit dwells in each man living the life of the Church, he is not limited to touching the surface of tradition but, in so far as he is filled with the spirit of the Church, he enters into it. But the measure of that spirit is also the measure of sanctity. This is why sanctity is an inner norm used to determine what constitutes Church tradition. The light of sanctity thus illuminates tradition.

From an exterior point of view, tradition expresses itself by all that is impregnated with the Spirit of the Church, and in this sense it is inexhaustible. Into the personal conscience of each member of the Church there enters only a drop of that sea, a grain of that treasure. But here, quality matters more than quantity. The timid and trembling light of a candle lit at the sacred flame preserves that same flame. The candles burning in the temple whose many lights transform themselves into one light represent Church tradition as diffused in the entire Church. In the interior life of the Church, its tradition assumes many forms, literature, liturgy, canonical documents, memorials.[1] All the life of the Church at all times in its existence, as far as it is fixed in documents—this is Church tradition.

Tradition is not a book which records a certain moment in the development of the Church and there stops, but a book always being written by the Church's life. Tradition continues always; we live in tradition and create it. And yet the sacred tradition of the past exists for us as present; it lives in our own life and consciousness. Moreover, between the past and the present there is this difference: that the present is for us fluid and without form, still being created, while the tradition of the past is offered to our knowledge in forms already crystallized, accessible to the mind.[2]

The hierarchy must be understood as an ordered, continuing charisma with a special purpose. Partly it is for the mystical transmission of the gifts of grace, for the succession

[1] Fr. edn: '*les monuments*', i.e., buildings and works of art. [Ed.]
[2] Bulgakov, S. N., op. cit., pp. 87 ff.

of life in grace. As a result of this, the hierarchy is bound up with the external fact of its succession; the hierarchy, not losing its charismata, becomes an institution, and thus into the life of the Church is introduced institutionalism, canonical law. But this institutionalism is of a very special nature, of which we must here take account.

Above all, and this is the most essential thing, the ministry is the power to administer the sacraments. Consequently it bears within itself that mysterious power, superhuman and supernatural. According to the testimony of ancient writings (Apostolic Fathers such as St Ignatius of Antioch) the bishop is he who celebrates the Eucharist, and only the Eucharist celebrated by a bishop is valid. The sacrament of the breaking of bread occupied at once the most important place in the Christian life. It became an organizing force in the Church, especially for the ministry. After Pentecost, the believers 'persevered in the doctrine of the Apostles, in the breaking of bread and in prayer'.[1] The central significance of the Eucharist in the life of the Church is attested by many documents of the first and second centuries. It was natural that, at first, the Eucharist should be celebrated by the apostles, and also by the charismatic leaders (the 'prophets' of the *Didache*) instituted by the apostles. But in post-apostolic times the administration of the sacrament of the Body and Blood fell to bishops alone. Little by little, in the usage of the Church, other sacraments were joined to the first. So the ministry, that is the bishops and the clergy dependent on them, was formed in the first place in connection with the power to administer the sacraments: it was a by-product of sacramental 'charismatism'.[2] This latter, being the foundation of the mystical life of grace in the Church, had to have its permanent representatives. The bishop, possessed of the fullness of charismatic power, naturally and inevitably became the centre around whom the whole life of the ecclesiastical community, which depended essentially upon him, turned.

It is thus easy to understand the logic of Christian thought

---

[1] Acts 2.42.

[2] Fr. edn: '*Donc la hiérarchie s'est formée tout d'abord en liaison avec la possession du pouvoir d'administrer les sacrements, comme une conséquence du c. sacramentel.*'

of the first centuries, from St Ignatius to St Cyprian. According to them, '*episcopum in ecclesia esse et ecclesiam in episcopo*'. From this charismatic foundation there came, in the course of the history of the Church, the development of later canonical law which defined the rights of the bishops in the Church, and, later still, the relations among the bishops. In the course of centuries, local and ecumenical councils regulated these mutual relations, which even now give evidence of the complexity of the situation at that time. The essential point is that the bishops, notwithstanding canonical differences due to historic circumstances, are entirely equal from the charismatic viewpoint: among them there never was a super-bishop, *episcopus episcoporum*, never a pope.

To appreciate properly the nature of the episcopal authority we must bear in mind its special features, arising from the nature of communion in the Church. It must be noted that in spite of its being often labelled 'monarchical', the authority of the Church is of quite a different nature from that of the state. It is a spiritual authority, which is above all a form of ministry.[1] In the use of his power the bishop works with the Church, but never above the Church, which is a spiritual organism, one of love. Agreement with the Church, and union with it, is the very condition of the existence of the bishop. This union cannot be expressed in terms of constitutional laws, whether those of democracy or of constitutional monarchy, because legal categories are not applicable here. If canon law is really law at all, it is a body of law *sui generis*.[2] The episcopal power may be even more absolute than that of an absolute monarch and still remain entirely latent and diffused in the union of the bishop with his people.[3]

To understand thoroughly the place of the ministry in the Church, we must think not only of the unquestionable prerogatives of the ministry, but also of those, no less unquestionable, of the laity. The laity are not merely passive subjects with their only obligation that of obeying the ministry; they are not in any way vessels empty of 'charism', or gifts, waiting

[1] Luke 22.26.
[2] Fr. edn: '*Si le droit canon est un droit, il est en tout cas un droit sui generis.*'
[3] Bulgakov, S. N., op. cit., pp. 57 ff.

to be filled by the ministry. The lay state should be considered as a sacred dignity; their baptism has made of them 'a people of God, a royal priesthood'. The significance of this idea, although it is sometimes exaggerated in Protestantism, even to the complete denial of the ministry, must never be minimized. As Christians having received baptism and the gift of the Holy Spirit through anointing, which may be conceived as a sort of ordination to the calling of Christian, the laity also are charismatic, though in a limited sense, especially in connection with the celebration of the liturgy and the administration of the sacraments. They can, in case of need, administer baptism. Finally, even in the sacraments whose administration is reserved to priests alone, particularly the Eucharist, the laity have a certain share. The priest, strictly speaking, cannot complete the sacrament alone, without the people. In other words, he administers the sacraments with the people, and the laity are co-administrators with him. In the spiritual organism which is the Church everything takes place in the unity of love, and not one organ can exist without the others. *Nonne et laici sacerdotes sumus?* Up to a certain point the words of Tertullian are applicable here.[1]

It is unthinkable that the mind of the Church, its self-awareness, should belong to one only among its members, to a ministry placed above the body of the Church and announcing to it the truth. A ministry placed above the people, that is, outside them, separated from them, is no more capable of proclaiming the truth of the Church than the people apart from the ministry or than a single isolated individual. In being thus separated from the Church and contrasted with it (*ex sese*) the ministry would be outside the Church and deprived of its spirit, for this spirit is union in love, and truth in the Church is given only in the measure of that unity. The pretension of the Pope to be the voice of the truth destroys the unity of the Church; it puts the Pope in the place of the Church: *l'église c'est moi.*

The same is true of the ministry considered as the collective episcopate. A guiding dogmatic principle is offered here by the Jerusalem Council of the Apostles from whom the ministry, in so far as it continues their ministration, continues the

[1] Ibid., pp. 60 ff.

succession. Strictly speaking, the succession of those gifts of the Holy Spirit given to the Church at the time of Pentecost and transmitted by the apostles to their successors extends to the whole Church. The 'apostolic succession' in the special restricted sense applies only to the sacramental ministry, the priesthood, and not to teaching and dogmatic consciousness. We see this exemplified in the Council of Jerusalem where there were assembled 'the Apostles and with them the elders', that is, the senior members of the community, people without high-priestly functions. 'Apostles and elders and brothers',[1] that is, the holy Apostles in union with elders and brothers, decided and gave their pronouncements together. The fact is significant, for here is exemplified all the positive force of the unity of the Church (Canon IV of the Council of the Vatican on the Church with its '*ex sese*' especially contradicts this fact), and in accordance with that union the assembly proclaimed: 'It has seemed good to the Holy Spirit *and to us*',[2] in other words, to the Holy Spirit which lives in us by our union.

Hence the question of an exterior organ of infallibility in the Church by its very form faces us with heresy: the idea of the Church—a spiritual organism whose life is unity in love— is replaced by the principle of spiritual power. This is heresy.

Here we touch the very essence of the Orthodox doctrine of the Church. All the power of Orthodox ecclesiology is concentrated on this point. Without understanding this question it is impossible to understand Orthodoxy; it becomes an eclectic compromise, a middle way between the Roman and Protestant viewpoints. The soul of Orthodoxy is *sobornost*,[3] according to the perfect definition of Khomiakov,[4] in this one word there is contained a whole confession of faith. Russian ecclesiastical language and theology use this term in a wide sense which no other language possesses; by it is expressed the power and the spirit of the Orthodox Church. What then is *sobornost*?

The word is derived from the transitive verb *sobirat*, to bring together, to assemble. From this comes the word *sobor* which, by a remarkable coincidence, means both 'council'

---

[1] Acts 15.23.   [2] Acts 15.28.
[3] Pronounced with the accent on the second syllable: *sobórnost*. [Ed.]
[4] Alexei S. Khomiakov, 1804–1860. [Ed.]

and 'cathedral church'. *Sobornost* is the state of being together. The Slavonic text of the Nicene creed translates the epithet *katholikē* when applied to the Church as *sobornaia*, an adjective which may be understood in two ways, each equally exact. To believe in a *sobornaia* Church is to believe in a *catholic* Church, in the original sense of the word, in a Church that assembles and unites: it is also to believe in a *conciliar* Church in the sense Orthodoxy gives to the term, that is in the Church of the ecumenical councils, as opposed to a purely monarchical ecclesiology. To translate *sobornost,* I have ventured to use the French word *conciliarite,* which must be used both in a restricted sense (the Church of the Councils) and in a larger sense (the Church catholic, ecumenical). *Sobornost* may also be translated as 'harmony', 'unanimity'. Orthodoxy, says Khomiakov, is opposed both to authoritarianism and to individualism; it is a unanimity, a harmonious sharing of authority. It is the liberty in love which unites believers. The word *sobornost* expresses all this.

This term evokes the ideas of catholicity and of ecumenicity, ideas connected but distinct. Ecumenicity means that the Church includes all peoples and all parts of the earth. Now this is the meaning that Roman Catholics generally give to the word 'catholicity'. A rather quantitative conception of catholicity (universal diffusion) has predominated in the West since St Optatus of Miletus (*c.* 366, *De schism. donat.* 2.2) and especially since Augustine (*De unit. eccles.* 2). In the East, on the contrary, catholicity is understood in a sense rather qualitative (cf. Clement of Alexandria, *Strom.* 7.17, and above all St Ignatius: 'Where Jesus Christ is, there is the Catholic Church', *Smyrn.* 8). Catholicity or *sobornost* may be defined qualitatively. That corresponds to the true meaning of this concept in the history of philosophy, notably according to Aristotle, where the adverbial phrase *to katholon* means 'what is so on the whole, or throughout', while *to kathekaston* means 'what is so in some instances'. That is Aristotle's version of the Platonic 'idea' or form, an 'idea' which exists, not by any means *above* things or, in some sense, *before* things (as in Plato), but *in* things, as their foundation and their truth. In this sense a Catholic Church means one which is in the truth, which shares the truth, which lives from the true life.

Then the definition *to katholon*, that is, 'in respect of the whole, throughout', shows in what this truth consists. It consists in union with the whole (*holon*), in the spirit of complete wisdom in the union of all.

In *sobornost* understood as 'catholicity' each member of the Church, equally with the assembly of the members, lives in union with the entire Church, with the Church invisible, which is itself in uninterrupted union with the Church visible and forms its foundation. So the idea of catholicity, in this sense, is turned inwards and not outwards. And each member of the Church is 'catholic' in as much as he is in union with the Church invisible, in the truth. Both the anchorites and those who live in the midst of the world, the elect who remain faithful to the truth in the midst of irreligion and general heresy, may be 'catholic'. In this sense catholicity is the mystic and metaphysical depth of the Church and not at all its outward diffusion. Catholicity has neither external, geographical attributes nor empirical manifestations. It is perceived by the Spirit which indwells the Church and searches the heart. But it must keep touch with the empirical world, with the Church visible. Catholicity is also conciliarity, in the sense of active 'taking counsel', of participation in the integral life of the Church, of life shared in the one truth.[1]

It must be remembered that even ecumenical councils are not external organs established for the infallible proclamation of the truth and instituted expressly for that. Such a proposition would lead to the conclusion that before or without the councils the Church was not 'catholic' and infallible. Apart from this consideration, the mere idea of an external organ to proclaim the truth would place that organ above the Church; it would subordinate the action of the Holy Spirit to an external fact, such as an ecclesiastical assembly. Only the Church in its identity with itself, its conciliarity, can testify to the truth that it knows. Is a given assembly of bishops really a council of the Church which testifies, in the name of the Church, to the truth of the Church? Only the Church can know. It is the Church which pronounces its silent, and sometimes not silent, Yes. It is the Church which agrees, or not, with the council's testimony to it. There are

[1] Bulgakov, S. N., op. cit., pp. 73–6.

not, and there cannot be, external forms established before-hand for the testimony of the Church about itself.[1]

The absence of any external, infallible authority in matters of doctrine, together with the possibility of relatively in-fallible definitions by ecclesiatical authority, expressing the catholic mind of the Church—this is the palladium of Ortho-dox liberty. It is at the same time the cause of the greatest astonishment: unto Catholics a stumbling-block and unto Protestants foolishness. The latter place above all the personal search for truth, a principle whose value cannot be over-estimated in Christianity; they cannot understand the necessity of placing their own subjectivity beneath the objectivity of the Church: of testing the former by the latter. For them the doctrine of the Church identifies itself completely with their personal opinions, or at least with the consensus of such opinions. Ecclesiastical tradition, kept by the whole Church in common, simply does not exist for them. But pro-ceeding from these ideas, it is possible to approach the idea of conciliarity, or at least there is nothing to stop it. The agreement of personal subjective opinions may be understood as the objective ecumenical truth, as its manifestation. Hence it is possible for Protestants, with their spirit of freedom, to understand Orthodox conciliarity as *sobornost*. As a matter of fact, Protestantism itself contains the idea of relatively infallible doctrinal authority. The assemblies and synods which fixed the professions of faith, such as the Augsburg confession, are nothing but ecclesiastical organs endowed with relatively infallible authority and accepted by the Church. And are not the centres for discussing disputes in the Church which are appearing in our day (the Lausanne Con-ference included) the start of a road ahead, not yet very clear from the dogmatic viewpoint, but already adopted in practice?[2]

Very often in questions of a secondary order, where Ortho-doxy offers only theological opinion or pious custom, the Roman Church presents either fully defined dogmas or at least officially approved doctrine—for instance, in the teach-ing about the future life in its various phases. Some may think that this is an advantage and that the absence of such

[1] Ibid., pp. 88 ff.   [2] Ibid., pp. 96 ff.

precision is a sign of weakness and immaturity. We do not deny this unfinished character, which finds its partial explanation in the historic destiny of Orthodoxy. But fundamentally this feature is inherent in the Church because its depths are inexhaustible. The finished character of a religious system does not always proceed from an interior maturity, but sometimes from the fact that everything in it has been hastily forced into the shape of serviceable formulae. This makes things easy for the weaker brethren but it fetters the Christian spirit, for this spirit is ever striving onwards and upwards. For 'where the Spirit of the Lord is, there is liberty' (2 Cor 3.17).[1]

In the sacraments the Holy Spirit is conferred, always and unchangeably, in a manner regulated by the Church, but it is received differently by different men. The Church has the power to invoke the Holy Spirit in the sacraments. Pentecost, which happened in the past for the assembled apostles, is always happening in the heart of the Church in the sacraments, thanks to the apostolic succession of the ministry. This is why the power to minister the sacraments is vitally connected with priesthood. Where there is no priest there are no sacraments (baptism excepted). This does not mean that, in such cases, the Holy Spirit is absent, for the way of the sacraments is not the only one which gives the Holy Spirit. The Spirit bloweth where it listeth, and the gift of the Holy Spirit is not confined to the sacraments, even in the Church. The gift of the Holy Spirit does not depend on human cognizance: no one knows whence it comes or whither it goes. In the sacraments of the Church, on the other hand, there is found a knowledge of, and a definite form for, the giving of the Holy Spirit. The Church possesses true sacraments, active sacraments; this is one of the signs of the true Church.

At first glance it may seem that the seven sacraments of Catholicism coincide with those of Orthodoxy: baptism, chrismation (confirmation), penitence, the Eucharist, the laying on of hands, marriage, unction for the sick. But is the coincidence perfect? This doctrine of the 'seven sacraments' has recently acquired the force of a dogmatic tradition in the Church. But it was formed only in the beginning of the

[1] Ibid., pp. 102 ff.

twelfth century, first in the West and later in the East. It must be remembered that the number seven has no limiting force, for the number of sacramentals (*sacramentalia*) in the Church is much larger. There are, for example, many special forms of blessing (of a church, of holy water, especially at Epiphany, then of bread, fruit, all objects); even funerals and monastic vows were once formally called sacraments. All these rites as well as many others, such as the consecration of crosses and ikons, do not differ from the 'seven sacraments' in what concerns their active force, for they also confer the grace of the Holy Spirit, when certain exterior forms are observed. The 'seven sacraments' are only the most important manifestations of the sacramental power inherent in the Church.

At the same time there is no reason why we should not distinguish even among the seven sacraments different degrees in their universality and even as to their divine institution, although all the sacraments are equally mysteries which confer the gifts of the Holy Spirit. But the Orthodox, together with Protestants, can set apart from the rest baptism and the Eucharist as instituted by our Lord himself and as being indisputable for all Christians. These are the 'sacraments of the gospel'. They have existed from the very beginning of the life of the Church. The other sacraments are also founded on words of Scripture, and, directly or indirectly, on words of our Lord, but they were only gradually established by the Church.[1]

It cannot be denied that Orthodoxy, not as the universal Church but as Eastern Christianity, wears an aspect which is less 'of this world' than that of the Christianity of the West. The West is more practical, the East more contemplative: Eastern Christianity considers as its first apostle the beloved disciple whom Christ from the cross gave as son to his Mother, the apostle of love. Western Christianity is especially filled with the spirit of the two princes of the apostles: Peter (Catholicism) and Paul (Protestantism). John wished to rest on the Master's breast, while Peter asked if two swords were enough and concerned himself with the organization of the Church. This explains the contemplative character of monastic life in the East. Here monasticism does not show the variety

[1] Ibid., pp. 180 ff.

and shades of difference evident in Catholic religious orders. Contemplation in the West is proper only to certain orders; in the East it is the characteristic trait of all monastic life. The monastic state in Orthodoxy is 'the acceptance of the angelic form', that is, the abandonment of the world for the service of prayer and ascetic practices, rather than for fighting in the world *ad majorem Dei gloriam*. Certainly the work of Mary and of Martha, the two sisters equally loved by our Lord, cannot be wholly separated, and still less can they be opposed; but there nevertheless remains a well marked difference. It is quite possible that Orthodoxy may now turn towards the world, more than it has ever done up to the present; the history of the Church seems to suggest it. But Mary still remains its spiritual type.

Orthodoxy has the vision of ideal spiritual beauty, to which the soul seeks ways of approach. Greek antiquity knew something of the same kind in its ideal of *kalokagathia* wherein the good and the beautiful are united. It is the celestial kingdom of those Ideas which Plato once contemplated: these are patterns in the angelic world, the spiritual 'heaven' which is reflected in earthly 'waters'.[1] It is a religious ideal, more aesthetic than ethical, an ideal which lies beyond good and evil. It is the light which brightens the way of pilgrims on this earth. This ideal calls us beyond the limits of our present life; it calls us to its transfiguration.[2]

We find a special difficulty for Orthodox ethics in a trait already indicated; the ideal foundation of Orthodoxy is not expressed in ethics, but is a matter of religious sensibility. It is the vision of 'spiritual beauty'; to gain it one must have a 'spiritual art', a creative inspiration. Such art remains the privilege of a small number; the others content themselves with morality which, by itself, has no 'spiritual flavour'. It does not inspire, it only disciplines. Neither that moralism of which we see an apotheosis in the rigorist and autonomous ethic of Kant, nor the practical 'probabilism' in vogue in Catholicism, really fits Orthodoxy. It cannot be denied that this spiritual aestheticism of Orthodoxy sometimes degenerates into indifference concerning practical necessities and above all the methodical training of the will. This has

[1] Gen. 1.1.   [2] Bulgakov, S. N., op. cit., pp. 175 ff.

unfortunately been evident in moments of historical crisis. Humility and love are the supreme characteristics of the Orthodox. From these qualities come the modesty, the sincerity, the simplicity which are so incompatible with the spirit of proselytizing, the authoritarian spirit (*compelle intrare*) which prevails elsewhere. Orthodoxy does not persuade or try to compel; it charms and attracts. Such is its method of working in the world.

Orthodoxy educates the heart; this is its characteristic trait, the source of its superiority and also of its weakness, which expresses itself in a lack of education of the will. The Christian ethics developed by the different confessions certainly reflect the differences existing between them. They are affected by the character of the different peoples and bear the mark of their historic destinies. Practical morality, philanthropy, form the domain where the division in the Christian world is least felt. And I think that, united in this, different Christian peoples, belonging to different confessions, may learn much from each other. The West may find a complement to its dryness in the free spirit of Orthodoxy; and the Orthodox East can learn from the Christian West many things in regard to the religious organization of everyday life. For Martha and Mary, while different in many ways, were equally loved by our Lord.[1]

In Christianity man is not only the intellectual but also the economic logos of the world, the master of creation. His is the right and the duty to work in the world for his own existence,[2] to aid his neighbour and to accomplish the common work of humanity,[3] in accordance with the precepts of God: 'Subdue the earth and rule over it'.[4] The work of man is a part of his link with nature, and to it the sanctifying grace of the Holy Spirit is joined. This abiding of the Holy Spirit in the world, through the Church, is expressed in the many things blessed by the Church—food, vessels, etc. In principle everything may be sanctified except those things which are employed with evil intention.

The sanctification of things needful to man and used by man is, in principle, of great importance; these are above all

[1] Ibid., pp. 179 ff.
[2] 2 Thess. 3.10.   [3] Matt. 15.   [4] Gen. 1.28.

the materials necessary to the ministration of the sacraments, the eucharistic bread and wine, the chrism for chrismation, and the oil for the unction of the sick, the waters for baptism. Afterwards there is the sanctification, by blessing, of wine, bread, fruits, oil, honey, and grain, the Easter dishes,[1] various objects, buildings, roads, etc. The Church thus gives its benediction to the elements of nature. This benediction extends to the entire domain of economic production and consumption. The sanctification includes a transfiguring power, so that man's activity which transforms nature, his economic toil, and the power of God which transfigures that nature, working above human power but not outside it, are wholly reunited.

All that has been said above determines the Orthodox point of view on economic life; we know that the history of Christianity always balances between two extremes: the renunciation of the world and the acceptance of time. It is indisputable that Christianity has freed and ennobled all labour, economic labour above all, and has given it a new soul. In Christianity is born a new economic man, and new motives incite him to work.[2]

In Christian eschatology the question is always present of the eternity of the pains of hell and the final reprobation of those sent into 'the everlasting fire, prepared for the devil and his angels'. From earliest times doubts have been expressed as to the eternal duration of these torments; they are sometimes viewed as only a provisional pedagogic method of influencing the soul, and a final restoration, *apokatastasis*, is hoped for. From the earliest times there have been two tendencies in eschatology: the rigorists affirm that suffering is eternal, final, and without end; the others, whom Augustine ironically calls the 'pitiful' (*misericordes*), deny the eternity of punishment and the persistence of evil in creation and acknowledge the final victory of the kingdom of God, when 'God shall be all in all'. The doctrine of *apokatastasis* is not only that of Origen, whose orthodoxy has been questioned because of certain of his opinions, but also of St Gregory of Nyssa,

---

[1] Eggs, pascha (a kind of cream-cheese), and kulich (a sweet loaf). [Ed.]

[2] Bulgakov, S. N., op. cit., pp. 193 ff.

glorified by the Church as *Doctor*, and his disciples. It has hitherto been thought that the doctrine of Origen was condemned at the Fifth Oecumenical Council, but recent historical studies do not permit us to affirm this. As to the doctrines of St Gregory, more thoroughly worked out and free from Origen's theories on the pre-existence of souls, they have never been condemned. Consequently they retain their standing in the Church, at least as theological opinions (*theologoumena*). It is true that the prevailing opinion set out in most Orthodox dogmatic manuals does not dwell on the notion of *apokatastasis* or even expresses ideas approximating to the rigour of Catholicism. On the other hand, certain thinkers have professed and still profess ideas influenced by the doctrine of St Gregory of Nyssa or at any rate more complex than the ordinary rigorist view. It may be thus foreseen that this question will often be raised again, and that it may become clearer as fresh light is given to the Church by the Holy Spirit. In any case, no rigorist view can take from us the hope afforded in the triumphant words of St Paul: 'God has shut all men up in rebellion, that He might have mercy upon all. O, the depth of the riches of the wisdom and of the knowledge of God' (Rom. 11.82–8).[1]

The Orthodox spirit, which pervades the universal Church, may be more apparent to the eye of God than to that of man. But at any rate all baptized persons are Christians, hence, in a certain sense, Orthodox. For Orthodoxy is composed, so to speak, of two circles: an outer circle, the court of the temple, and an inner circle, the temple itself and the holy of holies. Orthodoxy does not desire the submission of any person or group; it wishes to make each one understand. This is a field for the operation of the Holy Spirit indwelling the Church, beyond the direct efforts of men. Note here the sharp distinction between the attitude of Orthodoxy and that of Roman Catholicism. For the latter reunion means, first of all, submission to the papal authority. Orthodoxy does not value exterior submission. And if such submission is necessary, it is only for the purpose of settling matters of the canonical organization of the community joining in ecumenical unity, or to guard against the ambitious pretensions of a local

[1] Ibid., pp. 211 ff.

FBA

church, of which history affords examples. The ideal of the 'union of the Churches' in its contemporary form would be realized by the entry of all Christian communities into the heart of Orthodoxy, but only if the maximum and not the minimum of the common heritage of the Churches forms the basis of reunion. By picking out an abstract minimum on which all ecclesiastical societies would agree, unity could by no means be attained. This could only be a first step on the road.

Only a drawing together of the Churches, based on the maximum of their common heritage, can lead the Christian world to real union. This maximum is Orthodoxy. It cannot be a sort of amalgam or compromise, like a religious Esperanto, still less indifference to all dogmatic questions. Neither can it be something quite new in the history of the Church; for then all the earlier life of the Church would have been a mistake, a misunderstanding, a nullity. Orthodoxy is the interior way, the interior necessity for the universal Church on its way towards unity. It is only in Orthodoxy that the problems raised by the Christian confessions find a solution and an end, for it possesses the truth. Orthodoxy is not *one* of the historic confessions: it is the Church itself in its verity. It may even be added that, by becoming a confession, Orthodoxy would fail to manifest all its force and its universal glory; it would hide, one might say, in the catacombs.

The movement towards the reconstruction of universal Orthodoxy is steadily gaining force. In the same measure that the tendency of the sects towards isolation ceases, in the same measure that the ecumenical spirit is triumphing over sectarian Pharisaism, this movement is pressing forward, irresistibly, before our eyes today. It is not the result of Orthodox proselytizing, since there is no such thing. Contemporary Orthodoxy would probably not be able to muster strength sufficient for such a task, even if it wished. It is the Spirit of God who leads the peoples towards Orthodoxy, in spite of human frailty and narrowness. Indeed, what is the most important phenomenon of the spiritual life of the Christian world today? The search for the ecumenical Church, for integral unity.

This unity may be realized only in two ways: by Orthodox

conciliarity, *sobornost*, or by the authoritarian monarchy of Catholicism. The success and the conquests of ecclesiastical authoritarianism may be considerable now, and perhaps even greater in the future. But it may confidently be affirmed that the conquest of the Christian world by a religion of authority is an aim which cannot hope to be realized. If that should happen it would be a proof of reaction and of spiritual decadence. The world will not become Catholic. On the other hand, we observe that papalism is becoming more and more isolated in the Christian world. This fact became very clear with the appearance of the encyclical *Mortalium Animos* after the Conference of Lausanne. It must be noted, however, that Catholicism is something greater than papalism. It may well be said that the monarchy of the Vatican is a sort of shell, beneath which is the living body of the Church. And against the poisons of 'statism', of the juridical spirit, of ecclesiastical monarchism, which have affected that body, the ever-living organism of the Church is constantly metabolizing antitoxins. In spite of the triumph of authority in any Christian confession, the true mind of the ecumenical Church continues to live in the depths and naturally tends to another unity—an inner unity. This is witnessed by all the living holiness so plentifully manifested in Catholicism, not by virtue of but in spite of papalism. This is borne out again by the purely religious movements in Catholicism, such as the liturgical movement among the Benedictines or the 'Union' movement of the Belgian Priory of Amay.

The same tendency is much more clearly evident in the Protestant world. The two names of Stockholm and Lausanne symbolize the movement towards reunion, which has begun in the heart of the Christian world and which is already bearing fruit.

But this movement brings with it a re-examination and re-evaluation of the spiritual basis of the Christian communities. By the very force of circumstances, it leads irresistibly to more profound consideration of questions concerning ecclesiastical tradition, and in consequence, it leads to a return, at first almost imperceptible, towards Orthodoxy. This return is already evident in the advanced movements of the Protestant world, which designate themselves as

Hochkirchliche Bewegung. Thanks to the modern tendency to restore the plenitude of tradition, thanks to certain movements which are leading to the liberation of Catholicism from juridical overgrowths, an important trend towards Orthodoxy is becoming perceptible. But the decisive act, perhaps still far distant, would consist in the re-establishment of a ministry in the Apostolic Succession in those bodies where it was abolished.

A special place in this movement is occupied by the Episcopal Church of England, America, and other countries. I shall not touch here on the subject of the validity of Anglican orders, which is merely a canonical rather than a dogmatic question, to be decided for the Orthodox Church only by a competent ecclesiastical authority. In any case, the Episcopal Church is, of all the Protestant world, the nearest to Orthodoxy. Among the many tendencies in Anglicanism the Anglo-Catholic movement becomes more and more important. It is steadfastly bent upon the recovery of the old tradition and is drawing nearer to Orthodoxy. We may hope that the reunion of Orthodoxy and of the Episcopal Churches of England and America will be an accomplishment of the not too distant future, and that this movement will be a decisive phase in the re-establishment of the unity lost to the Church, and of peace between East and West.[1]

---

[1] Ibid., pp. 214–17.

The Comforter

Fifteen hundred years of logomachy about the procession of the Holy Spirit have not led to any positive dogmatic results. The problem remains dogmatically obscure in spite of the greatest efforts of thought; all the exertions of the scholastics, all exegetic and patristic studies, have proved fruitless. The lacework of subtle arguments grew apace, innumerable texts were piled up, but the only result was that the opponents set their teeth and, of course, in all good faith clung to their own opinions, each unable to convince the other. Attempts to overcome opposition not by the force of conviction but by the sheer weight of tradition have also led to nothing. This indeed was bound to be the case, since the patristic sources are not inexhaustible: they have been thoroughly explored, and they do not provide the desired answer in the sense of a clear, uniform, and unambiguous solution of the problem, which thus remains indefinitely suspended. The results for the life of the Church of the *filioque* dispute are entirely negative. A dogmatic question was used as a weapon for ambition, and in self-defence. This began with Patriarch Photius's first statement on the subject and was continued by the pride and ambition of Rome. At the Councils of Lyons and of Florence, aimed at the reunion of the Churches, *filioque* became the symbol of papal absolution or of its rejection (hence at the Florentine Council the Greeks were more concerned about the insertion of the *filioque* clause in the Creed than about the actual meaning of the dogma). In other dogmatic disputes ambitious, and in this sense schismatic, considerations also played their part, but they were never so completely identified with the dogmatic problems at issue as in this case. This primacy of schismatic motives, if one may put it so, in a dogmatic question about the Holy Spirit dooms the controversy to sterility, for where there is no will to union but only a desire for domination, the heart cannot be inspired to say, 'it seemed good to the Holy Ghost and to us'. In the history of dogma no instance can be found more remote from this 'seeming good to the Holy Spirit' than the disputes about the Spirit. But although six or seven centuries ago passions ran high in the heat of the controversy and the struggle for supremacy roused fierce resentment on both sides, at present the embers of the once blazing fire are covered with the ash of indifference. Although the old accusations of heresy are still exchanged between the disputants, neither side really believes in them any more. The judgement of an impartial historian which may in this case be regarded as the voice of dogmatic and critical conscience has already been pronounced: the *filioque* clause is not an unsurmountable obstacle to the reunion of the divided Church.

It is remarkable that the *filioque* dispute has destroyed all theological interest in the doctrine of the Holy Spirit. During the era of the Ecumenical Councils occupied with the problems of christology, the dogma of the Holy Spirit was not expounded and indeed remained neglected. The definition in the eighth clause of the Creed laid down by the Council of Constantinople simply recognizes the divinity of the Third Person as equal to that of the two other Persons. (This is expressed not directly but by implication.) It cannot by any means be regarded as an exhaustive dogma about the Holy Spirit. It remained unchanged, however, throughout the period that followed, so that in fact the *filioque* disputes, having no Spirit in them, proved to be an obstacle to true pneumatology. Carried on in the icy emptiness of scholastic abstractions, they never acquired the breadth and universality essential to real, significant pneumatology. True, they usually included more vital questions, e.g. about the descent of the Holy Spirit into the world from the Father and the Son, or from the Father through the Son; these problems, however, were considered not in themselves but merely as arguments in favour of this or that theory of the procession of the Holy Spirit, i.e., in fact were treated in such a poor, one-sided, and perverted way that, one may say, it would have been better if they had not been considered at all. (Of course this did not prevent dogmatic theology from expounding doctrine about grace, about the action of the Holy Spirit in the Church, about salvation, the Church, etc., but these expositions are always centred upon particular points of dogma and are never connected with or lead up to a general theory about the Holy Spirit.)[1]

Through the descent of the Holy Spirit there arises in the members of the Church what is called life in the Spirit. This is an entirely new reality, wholly dependent on Pentecost and impossible before it or apart from it. This fact is described in its different aspects in the Scriptures and in ascetic literature. But, however different its manifestations or shades of meaning may be, what is common to them all is that in spiritual life man receives something that transcends him, a supra-natural principle, which is assimilated by him and enters into his own life, making it both natural and supra-natural. What are the preconditions of spiritual life? In the first place, it is inaccessible to beings or entities which have not the gift of the Spirit in them, such as animals and lower creatures like plants and minerals. Further, the gift of the Spirit cannot be the achievement of human effort, however lofty, but presupposes the participation of the divine power overshadowing man. Socrates and Plato, Buddha and Lao-tsze as well as other righteous men and leaders of pre-Christian and non-Christian humanity, high as their spiritual level was, have no gracious life in the Holy Spirit. It is a case of qualitative difference, analogous to that laid down by Christ between John the Baptist, a greater man than whom there has not risen among them that are born of women, and the least in the kingdom of heaven who is greater than he (Matt. 11.11). This does not in any way invalidate the fact that man has a natural spiritual life which, having a basis in the divine Wisdom, may be called naturally gracious. It is on another level and must be distinguished from the gracious spiritual life, which is of a different kind, since it includes divine power. Grace is a supra-natural gift which may be given or withheld but cannot be replaced or acquired by anything human. This was made evident in the early Church, when grace was bestowed at the laying on of the apostles' hands.[2]

God who is in heaven is high and far off: he is as inaccessible to this world as heaven is to the earth, but this does not make

[1] Bulgakov, S. N., *Uteshitel* (Paris, 1936), pp. 161–3.
[2] Ibid., pp. 340 ff.

him alien and unknown to our world. Although God 'dwelleth in the light which no man can approach unto', he is known to this world, for 'the only begotten Son Which is in the bosom of the Father, he hath declared him', for 'he who hath seen the Son, hath seen the Father' by the power of the Holy Spirit. We know this unknown and inaccessible God, who is in heaven, for we know the Son through the Holy Spirit. The Father is not hidden but is revealed in them: he is not denied but revealed by their revelation. And this identification is not a cold, theoretical, intellectual conclusion but a living reality. No: for it is not only a revelation through the manifested, and therefore known, second and third Persons, but is the actual divine Self of the Father who reaches with his love the heaven of heavens and is personally present in the world, revealing himself to it in his own special way. The Person of the Father is not incarnate and does not come down from heaven but only sends the other two Persons; and this 'sending', which is the Father's love for those whom he sends and for those to whom he sends them, is his personal presence in love for us. He is celestially high and also terribly near in his personal love for every creature; he is God and Father, God the Father, the Father and God. There is no greater ontological nearness than that between the Father and the children, and there is no greater difference than that between the Source and Archetype of being and his created images.

This revelation of the Father of himself is the most consoling truth of religion, and at the same time it enables us to overcome all the difficulties of philosophical speculation. The Absolute is not the a-cosmic, empty, transcendent No, utterly unrelated to the world and therefore nonexistent for it, but is the Father, the transcendent and immanent, the unity of Archetype and images, related to the world. The transcendent Absolute ceases to be the bad, negative infinity forever receding into the emptiness of negation, but is a positive infinity correlating the absolute and the relative, divine and created being. Created being is posited by the Father in his own image which is the divine *Sophia*, God-manhood. The transcendent Absolute is not an impersonal and soulless objectivity incapable of relations with the world of personal spirits, and in its impersonality poorer than they are. The

Absolute is the Father, personal and absolute Spirit realizing himself in his tripersonal *sobornost* and going beyond it to the created spirits which he includes in the image of his personal soborny existence. The transcendent Absolute is not a dumb and blind will; it is not an arbitrary and despotic fate hanging over the world. God the Father is fatherly love, the sun of the world which is also its heart. It is of him that it is said: 'That ye may be the children of your Father which is in heaven: for He maketh his sun to rise on the evil and on the good, and sendeth rain on the just and on the unjust.'[1] The Absolute *loves*; it is the Father. This is the thought which unites in itself the absoluteness of the heavenly Father and the entire power of his revelation in the relative, and this power is love. Metaphysics finds complete satisfaction in this divinely revealed doctrine, for all its postulates are realized in it. And at the same time, it gives the only true and possible satisfaction to religious consciousness which needs God to be transcendent and heavenly, and yet close and accessible to us. The two things are combined in the revelation of God as Father, heavenly in his divinity and close to us in his father-hood.

All that we know and love in the Son is the Father, for such as the Son is, the Father is also. All the love and the inspiration which we have in the Holy Spirit is also the Father, for such as is the Father, such is the Holy Spirit proceeding from him; it is his own Spirit. In loving the Son and the Holy Spirit we love the Father, we know the Father, we contemplate his holy Person. If the Son and the Holy Spirit are love and the revelation of love, the Father is love itself, the very heart of love and, indeed, the will of love. We worship him as King and God, as almighty Creator, but in worshipping him with fear and trembling, we love him, the heavenly Father, the Father of heaven and earth, our Father. Together with St Paul we 'bow our knees unto the Father of our Lord Jesus Christ' and are his creation and his children.

'And count us worthy, O Master, with boldness, and unrebuked, to dare call upon Thee, God of heaven as our Father, and say: *Our Father who art in heaven! Abba, Father!*'[2]

---

[1] Matt. 5.45.   [2] Bulgakov, S. N., op. cit., pp. 445 ff.

The Wisdom of God

Anyone who has visited the church of St Sophia in Constantinople and fallen under the spell of that which it reveals will find himself permanently enriched by a new apprehension of the world in God, that is, of the divine *Sophia*. This heavenly dome, which portrays heaven bending to earth to embrace it, gives expression in finite form to the infinite, to an all-embracing unity, to the stillness of eternity, in the form of a work of art which, though belonging to this world, is a miracle of harmony itself. The grace, lightness, simplicity, and wonderful symmetry of the structure account for the fact that the weight of the dome and even of the very walls seems to dissolve completely. An ocean of light pours in from above and dominates the whole space below. It enchants, convinces, as it seems to say: 'I am in the world and the world is in me.' Here Plato is baptized into Christianity, for here, surely, we have his lofty realm to which souls ascend for the contemplation of ideas.

But as Plato's pagan *Sophia* gazes upon herself she learns to recognize herself in the divine *Sophia* and, indeed, this church is an artistic proof of her existence and of her reality, spread like a protecting canopy over the world. It represents the last, silent revelation of the Greek genius, bequeathed to the ages, concerning *Sophia*, the Wisdom of God. Yet this marvel of architecture, though designed in a theological age in obedience to the will of the emperor-theologian, remains without any obvious relationship to the theology of Justinian's epoch. It is a torch kindled for the benefit of subsequent ages. The dome of St Sophia crowns and as it were summarizes all the theological creativity of the epoch of the Ecumenical Councils. What is the inner meaning of this church of St Sophia, the Wisdom of God, which is like the swan song of the universal Church in the city of the new Rome? Is it merely a chiselled allegory, such as the churches dedicated to Peace, or Faith, or Hope? The building of this church is a definite landmark in the creative activity of the epoch. For from that time churches dedicated to Sophia began to be built both in Byzantium and in Slavonic countries, with a wealth of mysterious and elusive symbolism. Undoubtedly they are churches dedicated to Christ, but to Christ in the aspect of *Sophia*—to Christ-*Sophia*. What then does this imply? Byzantine theology as such has left behind no explanation of that to which this ecclesiastical architecture bears witness. It only bequeathed its hieroglyphic sophiology, as a theological problem, to the generations which succeeded it.

Nor was this theological problem taken into account or understood by old Rome, the *civitas Dei* as once the *civitas Romana*. There the universality of the Church was looked upon as a kind of spiritual citadel, the *imperium Romanum*, an organization of ecclesiastical authority culminating in the person of the Roman pontiff. The heavenly dome of St Sophia, which has been suspended as it were in mid-air, here came to rest on an hierarchical foundation. The dome was no longer the symbol of eternity but of finite limitation. Everything was now defined, determined, co-ordinated, and co-related under the supreme authority of Christ's representative on earth. Thus in the West the message of her pre-eminence enshrined in the churches of St Sophia was narrowed. In the East, on the other hand, such obstacles never existed. When the faith of Christ was first blazed abroad by the missionaries of Byzantium, there came to the northern land of the Russian tsardom (the 'Third Rome'), together with Christianity, this mysterious and as yet undisclosed revelation of *Sophia* enshrined in the hieroglyphics of ecclesiastical architecture.

The first capital of Russia, Kiev, 'the mother of Russian towns', was the first to adorn itself in the eleventh century with a cathedral of St Sophia. After this a growing number of churches was so dedicated as the Russian Church, and the influence of the state and of culture in general spread to the north. Moscow, the free city of Nijni-Novgorod, Yaroslavl, and other towns, began to build their own churches dedicated to *Sophia*, the Wisdom of God. Here, too, as in the past, the theological implications of this symbol remained long hidden as a sacred mystery, though there is some partial disclosure of them at this time. It is true that this does not apply to theology, which in the backward conditions of the nation at this period was practically non-existent, but only to the further development of sacred symbolism. The sophianic symbol was first disclosed to some extent in the establishment of the day of the feast of title. These festivals are associated with a different range of ideas from those of Byzantium. The churches of St Sophia in Russia, as a general rule, have their feasts of title on feasts of our Lady (in Kiev, the day of her nativity; in Novgorod and other places on the day of her Assumption). Secondly the texts of special services to *Sophia*, though not, it is true, very numerous, are highly significant. In this way we see that in the interpretation of *Sophia*, along with the Christological emphasis—which corresponds to the divine *Sophia*—there emerges another, mariological, emphasis, which corresponds to the creaturely *Sophia*, to the glorification of the creature. Even more significant are the sophiological symbols employed to depict divine *Sophia* in the theology of colour and imagery. Here the most complicated and involved dogmatic compositions, only with difficulty capable of definite interpretation, embody the devout contemplation of the unknown makers. These ikons have been accepted and authorized by the Church and are preserved to this day.[1] But these memorials of symbolic sophiology remain dumb, and though their meaning must have been clear at the time when they were composed, in our time, which lacks sophianic inspiration, they often remain enigmatic and partially incomprehensible relics of a former age. Scholastic theology commonly abandons the whole field of research into the lofty symbolism of sophianic churches and ikons, together with the appropriate texts of divine worship, to the realm of archaeology, as something essentially antiquated, or else interprets it somewhat unsympathetically as a theological misunderstanding, the result of the unduly elaborate allegorizing of Byzantium or its naïve imitation in Russia. All this wealth of symbolism has been preserved in the archives of ecclesiastical antiquities, but, covered by the dust of the ages, it has been of no use to anyone. The time has come, however, for us to sweep away the dust of the ages and to decipher the sacred

[1] See the photographs of ikons of *Sophia* in Van der Mensbrugghe, *From Dyad to Triad* (London, 1935).

script, to reinstate the tradition of the Church, in this instance all but broken, as a living tradition. It is holy tradition which lays such tasks upon us. It is a call neither to superstitious idolatry nor to rationalistic contempt, but rather to creative understanding and development. Our own particular time with its special revelations and destiny has a peculiar call to this task.

The theme of *Sophia* never had any place in western theology, either in the Middle Ages or at the period of the Reformation, in spite of the intense theological ferment of the time. Though there is no doubt that western theology constantly hovers on the brink of sophiological problems, yet the general context of the main problems of the Reformation and the Counter-reformation, with their exclusive emphasis on questions of personal salvation, of grace and of faith, was on the whole unfavourable to further dogmatic development, and particularly to a consideration of anthropology in its connection with cosmology, which is a special characteristic of sophiology. Protestantism showed itself particularly barren in this sphere, for it narrowed tremendously the whole range of theological problems. This is particularly true of modern Protestantism, both of the 'liberal' variety with its rationalistic adogmatism and historicism (*Leben-Jesu-Forschung*) and of the 'orthodox' variety, which reintroduces with new vigour all the limitations of its original world-view. Unfortunately the sophiological barrenness of western theology influenced eastern theology also in a negative direction, for, generally speaking, eastern theology was subject to influence from this quarter. Thus resulted a certain divergence between the true wisdom of the Church on the one hand and the rationalistic forms of theology on the other. Today we are compelled to re-establish the connection.

Quite unexpectedly and totally apart from any link with the eastern tradition of the veneration of *Sophia*, we observe the beginning of teaching on the *Jungfrau Sophia* in the West in the seventeenth century, in the doctrine of Jacob Boehme, the mysterious cobbler of Berliz. Boehme is perhaps the greatest genius among German thinkers. Together with Eckhart, he represents the secret dynamic of the philosophy of Hegel and Schelling, of F. Baeder and the romanticists. He had a tremendous influence on his contemporaries as well as on succeeding generations both in Germany and beyond it, for example, in England. In particular this applies to his peculiar doctrine of *Sophia* which is closely linked with his trinitarian theology. We may here add that an English mystic of the eighteenth century, Dr John Pordage, who wrote a series of remarkable treatises on *Sophia*, was thus influenced by Boehme's sophiology. This western interest in sophiology is primarily distinguished by the fact that already at an early stage it came to realize the vital nature of the problems involved and gave rise to a whole range of valuable and penetrating ideas on this subject. Nevertheless it cannot altogether be accepted by modern Orthodox sophiology, though this latter must give to it its due. The works of Boehme, Pordage, and others were diligently studied by Russian Freemasons at the end of the eighteenth and the beginning of the nineteenth centuries. The translations of these works, in spite of the prohibition of the censor, were published and read in Russia and undoubtedly had a lasting influence on Russian thought. However, modern Russian teaching on *Sophia* does not derive from these sources but from holy tradition, which silently pervades the whole history of the Eastern Church.[1]

The main purport of this essay is to expound the doctrine of *Sophia*, the Wisdom of God. This doctrine is at the present time responsible for a sort of ideological ferment even in our own Orthodox *milieu*. It has already evoked a hurried condemnation on the part of some of the hierarchy, in spite of the fact that the whole problem is only on the threshold of dogmatic consideration, as a result of the atmosphere of sensation or scandal thus created around the doctrine of the Wisdom of God. Though the western reader may already be acquainted with such words as *Sophia* and 'sophiology', for him these words are likely to be tinged with the peculiar exotic, Oriental flavour of *gnosis*, and indeed smack of every sort of rubbish and superstition. No one seems to suspect

---

[1] Bulgakov, S. N., *Premudrosti Bozhiei* (unpublished MS., 1936); Eng. trans. *The Wisdom of God* (London, 1937), pp. 13-21. Though the present text has been revised, the citations are to the English edition of 1937.

that in this controversy the underlying problem is one which
has a profound bearing on the very essence of Christianity,
that it is a problem which is even now being discussed by the
whole of western Christendom. The real point at issue is that
of the Christian vocation as it is related to the very nature
of Christianity; it is the problem of a dogmatic *metanoia*, of
nothing less than a change and a renewal of men's hearts.
The doctrine of divine *Sophia* has nothing to do with putting
forward any new dogma and certainly cannot be described as
a new heresy within Christianity, although such is the
attitude adopted by certain 'guardians' of the faith, who see
in complete stagnation the only guarantee of a true faith and
accordingly dread all new ideas.

Sophiology represents a theological or perhaps a dogmatic
interpretation of the world (*Weltanschauung*) within Christianity. It is characteristic only of one trend of thought within
Christianity; it is by no means dominant in the Orthodox
Church, in the same way as, for instance, Thomism or
'Modernism' is in the Catholic Church, or liberal 'Jesuanism'
or 'Barthianism' in the Protestant. The sophiological point of
view bears upon all Christian teaching and dogma, beginning
with the doctrine of the Holy Trinity and the Incarnation
and ending with questions of practical, everyday Christianity
in our own time; it offers a special interpretation. It is untrue
to affirm that the development of the doctrine of the Wisdom
of God leads to the denial or undermining of any part of
Christian dogma. Exactly the reverse is true. Sophiology
accepts all the dogmas acknowledged as genuine by the
Orthodox Church (though not those teachings which have
been accepted through scholastic misunderstanding and
frequently forced on the Church from outside). Wherein, then,
does this sophiological point of view lie, and in what way can
it be applied to the fundamental teaching of Christianity?
This essay is an attempt to give a short answer to the question.
The introduction can only indicate quite shortly the general
lie of the land.

The central point from which sophiology proceeds is that of
the relation between God and the world or, what amounts to
the same thing, between God and man. In other words we are
faced with the question of the meaning and significance of

God-manhood[1]—not only in so far as it concerns the God-man himself, the incarnate Logos, but precisely in so far as it applies to the theandric union between God and the whole of of the creaturely world, through man and in man. Within Christianity itself there is a never-ending struggle between the two extreme positions of dualism and monism, in a constant search for truth, which can only be found in the synthesis of God-manhood.

There are two opposite poles in the Christian attitude to life, which are both equally untrue in their one-sidedness. These are, first, world-denying Manichaeanism, which separates God from the world by an impassable gulf and thus makes the existence of God-manhood out of the question; second, an acceptance of the world as it is, combined with submission to its values, which is termed 'secularization'. We notice the former attitude in various, at times very unexpected, combinations, mostly in cases where a profound and serious religious attitude, a sense of the reality of God, confronts man with an either-or—either God or the world. Thus in choosing God man is constrained to turn away from the world, to despise its works and values, and to leave the world to itself and to its own endeavour in a state of alienation from God. We come across such a-cosmism or even anti-cosmism on the one hand, in a trend of thought which has historically prevailed in Orthodoxy—in the 'pseudo-monastic' outlook on the world and, on the other hand, in orthodox Protestantism which likewise so insists upon God's transcendence as to effectively deprive the world of God.

The second attitude or tendency—the secularization of life —is simply a symptom of the general spiritual paralysis of modern Christianity, which is, in practice, powerless to direct or to control life. Instead, it submits to the existing order of things. Such worship of the *status quo* shows that it has no answer to the problems of life. Moreover, if 'salvation' is

---

[1] This is the title which Vladimir Solovyev gave to his articles on sophiology—*Dissertations on God-manhood*. I have entitled my principal theological work in the same way—*On God-manhood*—Part 1: *The Lamb of God*; Part II: *The Comforter*; Part III: *On Things to Come* (ecclesiology and eschatology).

interpreted as a flight from the world and is at the same time associated with a servile attitude towards it we cannot be surprised that the world turns away more and more from such Christianity and comes to regard itself and its own life as capable of constituting its own standard of values. Such is modern atheism, which really represents a deification of the world and of men, and which is a special form of paganism. It is not—as it frequently claims to be—the nullification of religion, but a negation of Christianity.

Christianity is at present powerless to overcome this cleavage, this chasm between religion and the world, which is apparent in modern life, for the chasm exists not only outside but within Christianity itself. Attempts to co-ordinate Christianity with life (in so far as, in Roman Catholicism, this is accomplished on the basis of subjecting the world to a powerful ecclesiastical organization) are really nothing more than attempts to amalgamate two incongruous bodies which cannot in fact be united, since each insists on its own exclusivity or totality. 'Social' Christianity finds itself in the same tragic predicament in so far as it also represents an accommodation, a peculiar form of opportunism, without a dogma of its own. It strives to become an 'applied' Christianity, a 'Nicaea of ethics' to use the phrase of Archbishop Söderblom. But the very conception of 'applying' Christianity only confirms the absence of a genuine dogmatic Nicaea, together with a certain readiness to compromise with life, a retreat from it or a coming to terms with it, which is in no sense the exercise of creative leadership and inspiration for living. So far Christianity has followed in the train of life, lagging behind, without assuming any leadership. Furthermore, how can one lead in that which one does not accept, in which one does not believe, towards which one's attitude is merely that of missionary adaptation, of philanthropy, or of moralism?[1]

Our modern age stands in need of a new apprehension of the dogmatic formulae preserved by the Church in its living tradition. Moreover, it cannot be over-emphasized that there is no single dogmatic problem that does not at present need such reinterpretation. And at the very heart of things there stands, as of old, the basic Christian dogma of the Incarnation,

[1] Bulgakov, S. N., op. cit., pp. 27–33.

of the Word made flesh, in the dogmatic setting bequeathed to us by Chalcedon. The roots of this dogma penetrate to the very heart of heaven and earth, into the inmost depths of the Holy Trinity and into the creaturely nature of man. 'Incarnationism' even now stands as the main focus of dogmatic self-determination in Anglicanism and in Protestantism, as as well as in the more ancient Orthodox and Roman Catholic Churches. However, do people sufficiently realize that this dogma in itself is not primary but derivative? In itself it demands the prior existence of absolutely necessary dogmatic formulations concerning a primordial God-manhood. These presuppositions are in fact unfolded in sophiology. The same demand applies in an even greater extent to another dogma of God-manhood: namely, that of Pentecost. This dogma, though accepted, remains, comparatively speaking, feebly elucidated in Christian thought. It involves the descent and the abiding of the Holy Spirit in the world in connection with the Incarnation. This connection as well as the power of Pentecost in the one God-manhood is also disclosed by sophiology.[1]

Two forces struggle in the world in the guise of two basic tendencies, that of cosmism and that of anti-cosmism, the two disintegrated aspects of the one divine-human theocosmism. Historically, secularization was introduced into the world by the Reformation and the Renaissance, which represent two parallel turbulent streams of the same main current—of what we may call, however contradictory such a definition may sound, 'anti-cosmic cosmism'. The acceptance of the world by humanism was a reaction against its non-acceptance, which only left it a right to natural existence. We are confronted in this process by a bad 'dialectic' of unresolved contradictions, which burdens and exhausts our time.

But such a 'dialectic' in no sense represents the last word of wisdom. We need a true Christian *askesis* in relation to the world, which consists in a struggle with the world out of love for the world. We must discover how we can overcome the secularizing forces of the Reformation and of the Renaissance, not in a negative way or 'dialectically', which is in any case

[1] Ibid., pp. 35 ff.

merely theoretical and powerless, but in a positive way—through love for the world. But again I repeat that this can be accomplished only through a change in our conception of the world and through a sophianic perception of the world in the Wisdom of God. This alone can give us strength for new inspiration, for new creativity, for overcoming the mechanization of life and of man. The future of living Christianity rests with the sophianic interpretation of the world and of its destiny. All the dogmatic and practical problems of modern Christian theology and ascetics seem to form a knot, the unravelling of which inevitably leads to sophiology. For this reason, in the true sense of the word, sophiology is a theology of crisis—not of disintegration, but of salvation.

In contemplating a culture which has succumbed to secularization and paganism, which has lost its inspiration and has no answer to give to the tragedy of history, which seems in fact to have lost all meaning, we realize that we can find a spring of living water only by a renewal of our faith in the sophianic or theandric meaning of the historical process. As the dome of St Sophia in Constantinople with prophetic symbolism portrays heaven bending to earth, so the Wisdom of God itself is spread like a canopy over our sinful though still hallowed world.[1]

The tri-personal God has his own self-revelation. His nature, or *ousia*, constitutes his intrinsic Wisdom and Glory alike, which we accordingly designate under the general term *Sophia*. God not only possesses in *Sophia* the principle of his self-revelation, but this *Sophia* is his eternal divine life, the sum and unity of all his attributes. And here we must once and for all remove the common scholastic misunderstanding which makes of Wisdom no more than a particular 'property' or quality, comprised in the definition of God, and therefore devoid of proper subsistence. If this were so, then since *Sophia* is *ousia* revealed, the same consequence would follow for *ousia* as such. It too would lose its place in the substantial being of the divine Spirit and become no more than a 'quality'. Such an interpretation obviously impairs the dogma of the Holy Trinity. It would imply that God is a Spirit without a nature and that the divine hypostases are in fact devoid of

[1] Ibid., pp. 38 ff.

ousia. Their being would be confined to an abstract relationship of mutual self-abandonment, without any content of
nature, a conception akin to the *Ich-Philosophie* of the elder
Fichte.[1]

In opposition to this scholastic abstraction which can only
lead to heresy in regard to the doctrine of the Trinity, we must
insist on the full ontological reality of *ousia-Sophia.* Here is
no mere self-determination of the personal God, but *ousia,*
and therefore *Sophia,* exists for God and in God, as his sub-
sistent divinity. Yet no 'fourth hypostasis' is implied here;
we do not transform the Holy Trinity into a quaternity, but
recognize in the *ousia* the divinity of God, a reality 'other'
than his hypostases. It is quite natural, of course, for dis-
cursive reason to hesitate when confronted with the necessity
of drawing a distinction between the hypostatic and the
essential, sophianic being of the one self-sufficient divine
Spirit. Such a distinction, however, follows naturally from
trinitarian dogma, which is a doctrine not only of the hypostases of the Trinity but also of the consubstantiality of their
nature. No more will sound ontology suffer us to reduce the
essential nature of the Godhead to the shadowy existence of
a logical abstraction.[2]

The divine *Sophia,* as the revelation of the Logos, is the
all-embracing unity which contains within itself all the fullness of the world of ideas. But to the creature also God the
Creator entrusts this *all,* withholding nothing in himself and
not limiting the creature in any way: 'all things were made
by him [the Word]'.[3] In *Sophia* the fullness of the ideal forms
contained in the Word is reflected in creation. This means that
the species of created beings do not represent some new forms,
devised by God, so to speak, *ad hoc,* but that they are based
upon eternal, divine prototypes.[4] For this reason therefore the

---

[1] We can see a contrary error in the denial of personality in spirit,
leaving it no more than nature devoid of personal consciousness of self.
Such is the philosophy of the 'unconscious' in Schopenhauer, Hartmann,
and Drews.

[2] Bulgakov, S. N., op. cit., pp. 87 ff.

[3] John 1.3.

[4] The Platonic doctrine of ideas represents one philosophical form
of sophiology, which, however, finds no support in the revelation of
the tri-personal God. Cf. *The Light That Never Fades.*

world of creatures also bears a 'certain imprint' of the world
of God,[1] in so far as it shares the fullness of the divine forms
or ideas. This is clear from the fact that upon accomplishing
the work of creation God 'rested from all his work'.[2] This
similitude implies the exhaustive fullness of creation, the
twofold aspect of which involves both 'heaven and earth',
the world of angels and the world of men, and does not affect
the general postulate that the primary foundation of the
world is rooted in divine *Sophia*.[3]

Wisdom in creation is ontologically identical with its proto-
type, the same Wisdom as exists in God. The world exists in
God: 'For of him, and through him, and to him, are all things'.[4]
It exists by the power of his Godhead, even though it exists
outside God. It is here that we find the boundary which
separates Christianity from any kind of pantheism. In the
latter the world is identical with God, and therefore strictly
speaking neither the world nor God exists, but only a world
which is a god in process of becoming. In the Christian conception, on the contrary, the world belongs to God, for it is
in God that it finds the foundation of its reality. Nothing can
exist outside God, as alien or extraneous to him. Nevertheless,
as created from 'nothing', in this 'nothing' the world finds its
place. God confers on a reality which originates in himself an
existence distinct from his own. This is not pantheism, but
panentheism.

It is possible to ask: is not the creation of the world, as it
were, a kind of duplication of the divine *Sophia*? But the whole
conception of correspondence is inapplicable to the relation
between the eternal and becoming. Indeed, it is nearer the
truth to speak of unity, even identity, as between the divine
and the creaturely Sophia. At the same time, however, and
without equivocation, we can speak of the two different forms
of *Sophia* in God and in the creature. They are distinguished

[1] According to his favourite expression St Athanasius compares the
relationship between the created and the divine Wisdom (which in a
one-sided manner he identifies only with the Logos) with 'the tracing
of the name of the King's son on every building of the town which his
Father builds' (*Contra Ar.* 2.49).
[2] Gen. 2.1–3.
[3] Bulgakov, S. N., op. cit., pp. 106 ff.
[4] Rom. 11.36.

on the one hand as the simple and simultaneous perfection of eternity as against temporal becoming, and on the other divine, as against participated, being. The identity and distinction, the unity and duality of *Sophia* in God and in creation, rest on the same foundation.[1]

[1] Bulgakov, S. N., op. cit., pp. 114 ff.

The Apocalypse of John

The concluding words of the Revelation evidently belong to Christ: 'He which testifieth these things saith, *surely I come quickly.*' The words 'I come quickly' occur seven times in the Revelation and are repeated three times in the last chapter.[1] They conclude it with a special solemn confirmation, *nai erchomai taxu*, which is equivalent to 'yea, truly, amen'. These words are the main burden of the Revelation, the force of its promise. It was this promise that sounded so victoriously in the first preaching of Christianity—that set it aglow with fire, that comforted the martyrs and strengthened the confessors (e.g. Stephen's vision of Christ).[2] It expresses the world's brightest hope, and this is the secret of its victory in the world. It is impossible to state in human words all that it contains.

The Revelation begins and ends with the good news of the speedy coming of Christ. To whom then is the promise given? Is it only to the first generations of Christians, to the seer's contemporaries who in their simplicity and inexperience daily expected Christ's promised coming? They were very different from us, the sobered and disillusioned, who, tired of waiting, began as early as the second century to pray *pro mora finis* and later simply ceased to think about the *parousia*. The fiery Christian hope gave way to a lukewarm certainty that through being in the Church we already possess all fullness and need no dénouement. Some have found refuge in the fortress of the Vatican; others in less imposing fortifications, and in the all-sufficient grace of the sacraments, as if that grace were not a call but a kind of pleasant sedative. This has eventually led to a secret or open, passive or active struggle against the Book of Revelation: it was not read in church, and everything was done to neutralize it, either by a spiritualistic interpretation or by the critical method of the history of religions. In any case the thunder from heaven, 'Surely I come quickly',

[1] Rev. 22.7, 12, 20.   [2] Acts 7.

ceased to reach the Christian's spiritual hearing and indeed began to appear as a kind of misunderstanding, to be explained by the history of the Church. Certain mystically-minded and fanatical sects preserved an interest in the Book of Revelation, but they were obviously lacking in spiritual balance. How are we to understand this non-fulfilment of the most fundamental Christian prophecy, and what does it really mean? Does it mean that the time for it has passed, and it must be put aside (perhaps together with our faith) as no longer relevant? Or must we know without a shadow of doubt that the non-fulfilment of Christ's promise is unthinkable? It is addressed to all time and to all Christians without any exception both now and before and after, until we see Christ coming in his glory. 'Soon' is used here not in a chronological but in an ontological sense, giving a special colouring to Christian life as a whole, throughout time. Hence in Christian life 'those that possess become as though they possessed not', as though they had no continuing city here but sought one to come.[1] Christ's promise is at the same time a fulfilment, having power and authority. It should always be kept in heart and mind as a transcendent manifestation of the life of the world to come. The consciousness of this should be the central and most essential thing in our life, the highest and most indubitable spiritual reality. This is Christianity; this is our faith and the substance of it. A non-apocalyptic, non-eschatological Christianity is a dangerous counterfeit of the real thing and a secularization of it. It is in order to rouse and strengthen this consciousness in us that St John's Apocalypse has been given to us, with its promise, 'surely I come quickly'—'the Lord which is, and which was, and which is to come, the Almighty'.

He which is to come comes to 'his own': he comes to our world as a whole and to every one of us. If there is One who comes there must be one who meets him, and every Christian is called to this meeting. This is why the last promise of Revelation is followed by the answer of faith, by the acceptance of the promise: 'Amen, even so, come Lord Jesus.'[2] 'Amen' is the answering yea to the silent question contained in the Lord's promise: do you want me, do you accept me?

[1] Heb. 13.14.   [2] Rev. 22.20.

The question is addressed to every one of us, and the answer must also be given by everyone personally. This 'amen' must express our hearts' turning towards that promise, the *metanoia* to which men were called by the preaching of John the Baptist: to turn from the world to the Lord.

The answer must not only consist in a passive acquiescence, but be actively realized in the prayer: 'Come, Lord Jesus'— the most fervent, the most universally Christian prayer. The Lord teaches us to pray 'Our Father . . . Thy kingdom come', which is the deification of the creature in Christ by the Holy Spirit. Here it is the same prayer, but it is more precise and urgent: that which is most terrible, the Last Judgement which makes our hearts tremble, is the actual subject of the prayer—the first and for a long time the only Christian prayer. We fear the Apocalypse, hide it from ourselves in various ways and hide ourselves from it, because it calls us to that last and awesome prayer, *Maranatha!* Even so, may the Lord come!

Once again it must be emphasized that this prayer and the call to make it are addressed not only to those early Christian communities which were to receive the Apocalypse as a pastoral epistle (to seven particular churches, but through them to the whole Church). It is addressed with equal force to all churches, and to all of us now, to every last one of us. St John the Divine utters for us and together with us the great 'amen', and the resounding prayer: 'Even so, come!' And this must be not only a spoken but a living, burning prayer, giving us a lively hope and certain knowledge of him who is to come.

But the fire of faith which this prayer expresses has completely gone out in us. We never use this prayer of prayers. It is not in our Prayer Books. We pray to the Holy Spirit to 'Come and dwell in us'. We are up to that, because we understand this as his partial coming, as his gracious help in our infirmity—which help, however, leaves us essentially as we were before. But by the prayer to our Lord Jesus, 'Even so, come!', nothing half-way can be meant. Things will not be left as they were, life will not be left unchanged. (The same applies to the 'Jesus Prayer' which we have come to love for ourselves alone, as a prayer for the forgiveness of sin and for our personal salvation, with no more precise implication.)

Our Lord Jesus Christ himself gave us another 'Jesus Prayer': his own, which we have forgotten, if indeed we ever truly knew it.

But now the time is coming, indeed is already at hand, when these words of our present Saviour and coming Lord shall begin to glow for us with a new fire. They shine with a new inspiration and demand from us a living 'amen'.

Having once heard this call we cannot hold aloof from it; and we do not wish to do so. Even so, come! is a personal call to Jesus. (Thus used, his name occurs only once in the Revelation.) The personal call in the non-apocalyptic prayer to Jesus loses to a certain extent its personal character through its very length: 'Lord Jesus Christ, Son of God, have mercy upon me.' But here, in the Revelation, it is as it were a personal 'thou' addressed by mankind to the God-man. It renders the prayerful expectation of the coming Christ even more direct and real. The Revelation shows the figure of Christ, whom we know from the gospel, in a light which shines nowhere else; this 'view from the way to martyrdom' is marked too in the last occurrence of the apocalyptic prayer of prayers: 'Come, Lord Jesus. Amen.'

This is the last word of Revelation. It is followed only by the apostolic blessing, usual in all apostolic epistles. The Book of Revelation was one of them. The blessing, which is differently worded in the various epistles, is here given in its shortest form. It is bestowed in the name of Jesus only: 'The grace of our Lord Jesus Christ be with you all. Amen' (Rev. 22.21).[1]

[1] Bulgakov, S. N., *Apocalypsis Ioanna* (Paris, 1948), pp. 262-5.

7

An American Sermon: 1934

Abridged from the *Hale Memorial Sermon of 1934*, preached by Father Bulgakov in the Chapel of Seabury-Western Theological Seminary (a theological college of the Protestant Episcopal Church), Evanston, Illinois, on 7 November 1934. A copy of the complete text is in the Bodleian Library, Oxford.

Social Teaching in Modern Russian Orthodox Theology

It is to be noted that the Orthodox countries have belonged to the stagnant and backward parts of the world in the economic sense. They were principally agricultural countries with feebly developed industrial life. Natural and domestic economy prevailed. The slavery of the first centuries of our era gradually disappeared, partly through the influence of Christianity, but was followed by serfdom, which was severe enough even though mitigated by personal relations and customs, such as were described by Carlyle in *Past and Present* and by the Russian writers Turgenev and Tolstoy. Yet even in this torpid existence doubts arose about the justice and value of such a tenor of life, which seemed to be unchangeable. The attitude of the Church was ascetical and conservative, following the commandment of St Paul: 'Let every man abide in the same calling wherein he was called', so that he might be a good slave for the sake of God, or a good lord for the sake of God.[1] Peace and quietness of soul were esteemed more highly than any economic striving. It is quite characteristic that one of the most renowned bishops of the Russian Church in the first half of the nineteenth century was not favourable to the emancipation of peasants, although he later became the author of the text of the tsar's manifesto granting such emancipation.

The asceticism of the first ages of Christianity has been the prevailing and even chief factor determining Christian social doctrine, or what we may call Christian sociology. Poor people have to endure their destinies for the sake of God, and rich people have a responsibility to use their wealth according to the teaching in the parable of the rich man and Lazarus. Reconciliation with the existing social order, sometimes even of a worse kind than that of the first century, was a natural

[1] 1 Cor. 7.20.

consequence of such a world-view; the Communist hatred of religion which finds its expression in the phrase, 'Religion is the opiate of the people', is a practical sequel to this quietism, this social nihilism.

Social life became paganized, and even this fact of paganization itself put a new question before Christian doctrine, like the riddle of the Sphinx: 'Answer me or I shall devour you.' Personal, individualistic Christianity remains in any case a necessary side of Christian doctrine and life, in as much as Christianity is a religion of salvation which is a personal adoption of the redemption given by Christ, our Saviour and Lord. This redemption is given by Christ as the High Priest who gave himself as a sacrifice for the remission of sins. Each Christian soul has its own personal relation to Christ by the adoption of this forgiveness, its own way in the fight against sin. Each separate personality is a single reality from the point of view of redemption. But the question arises, whether the whole reality of human life is exhausted by these separate personalities or whether there exists in addition humanity as a whole, as an organism? How are we to understand the life and history of the world and of mankind in this sense?

The world belongs to man, who is its head. This basic principle is not altered, whether by original sin or by salvation from it through Jesus Christ. In a certain sense, in the incarnation of Christ the world itself became the Body of Christ. It is glorified and transfigured in Christ through the Holy Ghost in his own life, but this life contains in itself the whole of humanity, which is to be glorified and transfigured. Here we find an analogy with personal salvation, which is given and accomplished through the sacrifice of Christ, yet has to be adopted by personal ascetic effort. And the salvation or the transfiguration of the world which is already achieved by Jesus Christ through the Holy Ghost has now to be accomplished from the human side by the sons of God. The road to salvation, and in this sense to the end of the world, must now be trod also by mankind, by the sons of God. The end of the world in this sense is not only the inscrutable will of God which is known neither to angels nor even to the Son of Man, but it is an end to be prepared and reached by human history as well. We may express this idea in the term Christian humanism, which is the opposite of the godless humanism of modern times. All these human, creative endeavours must be made in the name of Jesus Christ; being inspired by the Holy Ghost, Pentecost is continued in them.

Christian humanism, which presumes the development of all the creative capacities of man, may be understood as a new comprehension, a new revelation of Christianity. It is no new Christianity; it is only its new comprehension. The various new dogmatic definitions given by the Church from time to time have been new comprehensions of the same Christianity. They were accepted as true answers to questions raised by the leaders of heresy. For instance, Arianism was such a question, and the Nicene Creed was the answer of the Church. And now false, atheistic humanism is a question put to the Church, and Christian humanism would be an answer. The leading idea of this creative apprehension of Christianity is that there exists in history, to use the expression of the Russian philosopher Feodorov, a 'common work' for human brotherhood. This common work or task has no exterior limits; it embraces the whole world and involves the overcoming of the blind forces of nature and the accommodation of them to human will and tasks, as well as the appeasing of elementary social forces. Social life is to be organized according to the postulates of Christian love, so also the whole of political life. At present we have not only the separation of the Church from the State —which means the freedom of the Church and is even favourable for her life—but the general secularization of life, its paganization. To meet this situation we must seek for a state of things in which the Church may penetrate as with inward power the whole of human life. The separation of the Church from life must at last be overcome, and all sides of the natural existence of men—certainly all except sin—are to be included in the grace-abounding life of the Church. This postulates of social Christianity or of Christian humanism a new dogmatic generalization or a new understanding of the incarnation. It is the general principle of social philosophy which must be developed and applied to different sides of life.

The developing of this postulate is, I believe, the chief achievement of modern Russian theological thought. As a doctrine it is not yet sufficiently developed; it is a dogmatic postulate rather than a completed programme of life, prophecy more than actuality. But it opens a new way for Christian life and for Christian history. It gives to it not only a negative, but a positive sense; it includes the creativity of man in the means of his salvation. It does not deny Christian freedom from the world and the value of a spiritually ascetic way, or the fight against sin in the life of every man, but it calls all to work also for this world. It does not teach us to love this passing world, which is destined for the fire, but to love this world as the creation of God, who himself loves it. Particularly this Christian humanism contains the dream of all Christian youth, prophetically realized in the life of the community in Jerusalem, when all lived together in love and had all in common. This life of the Christian family, which has been called a Christian 'communism' or 'socialism', remains a guiding star on our horizon. The Christian life cannot be limited to an individualistic life; it is common or social, yet without violating the principle of Christian freedom. It must be unity in freedom and love. The glorified body of the risen Christ was transparent to the spirit; it was a spiritual body, being at the same time no spirit but a body which could be touched, and this transparency was its glorification and beauty.

The same ideal of the transfiguration of the inert and dark matter of the world, its obedience and transparency to the spirit of man, is the final task of the creativity of man, who is called by God to have dominion over the world.

8

Festival Sermons

Five sermons of Father Bulgakov selected to
represent his preaching on major themes of
the Christian year.

The Power of the Cross

From a sermon preached by Father Bulgakov on the
Feast of the Exaltation of the Holy Cross, 14 September 1924.

Today the Lord's cross is raised before all the world; today
'the cross is raised and the world hallowed', and the faithful
are called to worship the thrice blessed tree on which Christ
was crucified. We pray to the tree of the cross, and we pray
to the holy life-bearing cross itself, we invoke it, we call to it:
'Thou art my mighty defence, tri-partite cross of Christ,
hallow me with thy power that I in faith and love may worship
thee and glorify thee.' 'Rejoice, life-bearing cross, unhindered
victory of godliness, the door of paradise, the confirmation of
the faithful, the defence of the church ... impregnable armour,
bane of devils ... bestowing mercy upon the world.' 'O cross
of Christ, thou hope of Christians, teacher of those in error,
haven of the storm-tossed, victory in battle, pillar of the
universe, physician of the sick, resurrection of the dead, have
mercy upon us.' 'Those who rely upon thee, O thrice blessed
and life-giving cross, rejoice together with the heavenly hosts.'
'Invincible, unfathomable and divine power of the life-giving
and honourable cross, do not forsake us sinners.' 'O glorious
and life-giving cross of the Lord, help us together with our
Holy Lady the Mother of God and all the saints, world without
end. Amen.'

But however much we may revere the actual precious
and life-bearing cross of the Lord, surely we are not tree-
worshippers who pray to a tree as to a living being, as to an
intelligible essence? Is it to a tree, even if it be thrice-blessed,
that we pray, or to the divine power and mystery of the cross
manifested to us in that tree? Worship of Christ's cross is
indeed inseparable for us from the worship of the cross abiding
in heaven, a divine and unfathomable power. The earthly
cross leads our minds to the contemplation of its archetype,
the heavenly cross, as indivisibly united to it as the divine and

the human natures are indivisibly but without confusion
united in Christ. The heavenly cross of the Lord shone forth
on earth in the tree of the cross, the instrument of our
salvation.

At the creation of the world the seed of trees for the cross
was planted in it—the cedar, the oak, the cypress; on the day
when the earth was bidden to bring forth every kind of plant,
the trees for the cross sprang up. But the cross made of wood
is the symbol of the eternal cross, the revelation of the
mystery of the cross. The sign of the cross is written upon the
world as a whole, for, in the words of the Church anthem, it is
the 'four pointed power' binding together the 'four corners of
the world' as 'height, breadth and depth'. It is written too
in the image of man with his arms outstretched: Moses and
Joshua praying with their arms uplifted prefigured the
Crucified. The form of the body calls forth, as it were, the
tree of the cross, for it is itself a cross, the centre of which is
the heart. In the image of the cross the Creator inscribed his
own image in the world and in man, for according to the
testimony of the Church, the cross is the divine image im-
printed upon the world. What does the sign mean? It proclaims God's love, and in the first place God's love for his
creation. The world is created by the power of the cross, for
God's love for the creation is sacrificial. The world is saved by
the cross, by sacrificial love; it is blessed by the cross and
overshadowed by its power. But the mystery of the cross is
even more profound, for it wondrously contains the image of
the tri-personal God, of the Trinity in unity. The Church
teaches that it is the symbol of the unfathomable Trinity,
the three-membered cross bearing the tri-personal image of
the Trinity. The cross is the revelation of the Holy Trinity,
and the power of the cross is a divine power. When we call in
prayer upon the incomprehensible, invincible, and divine
power of the precious life-giving cross, we pray to the Source
of life, the Trinity in unity, one and divine in life and substance. The cross is God himself in his revelation to the world,
God's power and glory.

God is love, and the Holy Cross is the symbol of divine love.
Love is sacrificial. The power and flame, the very nature of
love is the cross, and there is no love apart from it. The cross

is the sacrificial essence of love, since love is sacrifice, self-surrender, self-abnegation, voluntary self-renunciation for the sake of the beloved. Without sacrifice there can be no acceptance, no meeting, no life in and for another; there is no bliss in love except in sacrificial self-surrender which is rewarded by responsive fulfilment. The cross is the exchange of love, indeed love itself is exchange. There is no other path for love and for its wisdom than the path of the cross. The Holy Trinity is the eternal cross as the sacrificial exchange of Three, the single life born of voluntary surrender, of a threefold self-surrender, of being dissolved in the divine ocean of sacrificial love. The tri-partite cross is the symbol of the Holy Trinity. How is this true? In the cross three lines meet and intersect; they approach one another from different points but as they intersect they become one in the heart of the cross, at their meeting point. Similarly in the Holy Trinity the divine life of the Tri-unity is an eternal meeting, exchange of self-surrender and of self-discovery in the two other Hypostases. No limits can be set on love or sacrifice. Renouncing oneself in order to live again in the other—such is the bliss of love. He who loves another loves the cross as well, since love is sacrificial. Love itself, God, in the eternal cross surrenders himself for the sake of his love. The three points in which the lines of the tri-cross end are images of the three divine self-subsistent Hypostases, and the point of their intersection is the co-inherence of the three, the Trinity in unity in sacrificial exchange.

The bliss of divine love is the sacrificial bliss of the cross, and its power is a sacrificial power. If the world is created by love, it is created by no other power than the power of the cross. God who is love creates it by taking up the cross in order to reveal his love for the creature. The almighty Creator leaves room in the world for the creature's freedom, thus as it were humbling himself, limiting his almightiness, emptying himself for the benefit of the creature. The world is created through the cross of God's love for the creature. But in creating the world through the cross, God in his eternal counsel determines to save it, also through the cross, from itself, from perishing in its creatureliness. God so loved the world that from all eternity he gave his only begotten Son to be sacrificed on the cross to save the world and call it to eternal life through the death of the cross and resurrection. God seeks in the creature a friend, another self, with whom he can share the bliss of love, to whom he can impart the divine life, and in his boundless love for the creature he does not stop at sacrifice, but sacrifices himself for the sake of the creature. The boundlessness of the divine sacrifice for the sake of the world and its salvation passes all understanding. The Son humbles himself to become man, taking upon him the form of a servant and becoming obedient unto death, even the death of the cross. The Father does not spare his beloved, his only-begotten Son, but gives him to be crucified; the Holy Spirit accepts descent into the fallen and hardened world and rests upon the Anointed, Christ, dwells in his Mother, and sanctifies the Church. It is the sacrifice not of the Son alone, but of the consubstantial and indivisible Trinity as a whole. The Son alone was incarnate and suffered on the cross, but in him was manifested the sacrificial love of the Holy Trinity— of the Father who sends him, and of the Holy Spirit who rests upon him and upon his sorrowing Mother. The cross was prepared in the world by God for God and was therefore prefigured in the Old Testament by many symbols and images. And the cross appeared to the world as the salutary tree, as victory over the world; hence the sign of the cross will victoriously appear in heaven at the second and glorious coming of the Son of God, and in the heaven of heavens there ever shines the Holy Cross, the vision of which was vouchsafed to St Andrew.

Demons tremble at the blessed sign of the cross. The cross is to them a consuming fire. Why do they tremble at this fire of love? Because they hate love, because they are darkened by selfishness and cannot abide the path of the cross; they are united in their legions by the power of common hatred and not of love. The cheering and comforting fire is to them an unendurable flame.

The cross is the figurative inscription of God's Name, working miracles and manifesting powers, like the Name of God revealed to Moses. The cross is the symbol of the Holy Trinity, the sacred sign of God who is love, burning up enmity, malice, and hatred.

This heavenly cross has been revealed to us men in the cross of Christ, in the blessed tree the image of which we worship and kiss with awe. We are signed with it as soldiers of Christ, we wear it on the breast and carry it in our hearts. A Christian is essentially a cross-bearer. The sweetest Name of Jesus is said to have been inscribed on the heart of St Ignatius of Antioch, the God-bearer; and similarly the heart of a Christian holds the cross of the Lord which has pierced it once and for all and set it aglow. A Christian lives in God, and, in so far as he enters into the love of Christ, he shares both in the burden and in the sweetness of his cross. To worship the cross and to glory in it is for him not an external commandment, but an inner behest: 'Whosoever will come after Me, let him deny himself, and take up his cross, and follow Me.' We can only worship the cross to the extent to which we share in it. He who is afraid of the cross and in his inmost heart rejects it worships it falsely and deceives his own conscience. This is why today's feast is both sweet and terrible, and the Church accompanies its celebration with a strict fast. The cross shines in the sinful darkness of our heart, illumining it and at the same time exposing it. Our sinful, self-loving nature fears it and resists it. Why deceive ourselves? The natural man is afraid of the cross. And yet we must overcome this fear; we must bring forth the tree of the cross in our hearts, lift it up, and worship it. We must lay on our shoulders, too, as did Simon, the Cyrenian passer-by, the burden of Christ's cross. Everyone must take up his cross and never leave it, and, raising the cross in his own soul, help to raise it in the world.

The Saviour's commandment to bear one's cross is not a harsh infliction of pain, but God's great mercy towards man. It is a sign of God's love for man, of great respect for him. God wants his highest creation to participate in his cross, in his joy and bliss. It was vouchsafed to Adam while still blissfully ignorant of good and evil to taste the sweetness of the cross through obeying the divine command not to eat of the fruit of the tree of knowledge. The tree of life and the tree of knowledge grew together in the garden of Eden.[1] That was the paradisal sign of the cross: renouncing his own will and doing the will of the heavenly Father, man was crucified on

[1] Gen. 2.9.

the tree which became for him the tree of life, full of eternal
bliss. But, through the whispering of the wily serpent, Adam
and Eve rejected the cross; they came down from it having
willfully disobeyed. And the tree became deadly for them and
gave them knowledge of good and evil, which entailed exile
from paradise. But the new Adam, the Lord, the Son of man
and only-begotten Son of God, ascended the cross which the
first Adam had forsaken; he was lifted up on the cross so as
to draw all men unto him,[1] for there is no way except that of
the cross to the sweetness of paradise. The ancient serpent
tried to tempt him too, saying to the Crucified through the
mouth of his own servants: 'Come down from the cross!' But
the new temptation was rejected, and the tree of knowledge
became once more the tree of life, a life-bearing garden, and
those who taste its fruit partake of immortality. In every
man so long as he lives there lives the seed of the old Adam;
he hears the unceasing whisper seconded by his natural
frailty and infirmity: 'Come down from the cross, don't
torture yourslf.' The world wars against the cross, is driven
to fury by the preaching of the gospel; love of the world is
hatred of the cross. But love of God is also love of the Lord's
cross, for our hard, rebellious heart can only love if it be
pierced by the cross. Sweet are thy wounds to my heart, O
most sweet Jesus, and it knows of no greater sweetness!

*O Glorious Miracle, the width of the cross matches the breadth
of heaven, since divine grace hallows all. Amen.*

---

[1] John 12.82.

The Doors of Penitence

Open to me the doors of penitence, O Life-giver![1]

The Church is praying today for the opening of the doors of penitence. What are those doors? Where are they to be found? How often we complain and bewail that we know no repentance, that we cannot and do not know how to repent! The heart remains cold and empty even when we seek repentance, and our mind remains drowsy. And yet we know that without repentance there is no salvation. Apart from it we cannot draw near to God's kingdom; there can be no living faith without it. It is the salt of faith. How are we to enter into the force of it?

Repentance begins by consciously seeing and knowing our sin: 'for I acknowledge my transgressions, and my sin is ever before me'—this is how the soul testified of itself in the Psalmist's penitential lamentation (Ps. 51).[2] A man may not be conscious of his sin at all, being in complete bondage to it. The soul may be sunk in deep death-like sleep, and if it does not wake the sleep will prove to be the sleep of real spiritual death. So long as men remain unconscious of sin, they hate in their heathen blindness the very word 'sin' and feel angry irritation at the thought of it. The soul is vaguely aware that it means condemnation of its whole past and a call to renewal: 'Repent ye and believe the Gospel' (Mark 1.15)—and our selfishness and inertia resist that call. Without repentance the natural man cannot be born as a spiritual man. So this is the first door of repentance: knowledge of one's sin and of oneself as possessed by it. A ray suddenly lightens the soul's darkness, and in its light man sees himself before the face of God. The eye of God beholds us through our conscience, which is God's testimony of himself in the soul of man. Conscience judges us with true, righteous, and uncorrupt judgement, and its present

[1] From a prayer in the *Triodion* (Lenten hymns and prayers) for Matins on the fourth Sunday before Lent. [Ed.]

[2] The prayer quoted above follows Psalm 51 in Matins. [Ed.]

judgement is as it were an anticipation of Christ's Last Judgement. It is the greatest gift of divine love which God has bestowed on man, for what can be 'more needful than conscience'? (in the words of the Great Canon of St Andrew of Crete).[1] Through conscience we see ourselves in the light of divine truth: 'that thou mightest be justified when thou speakest and be clear when thou judgest' (Ps. 51). This priceless gift of God is entrusted to everyone, not only to Christians, but to the Gentiles as well. The first impulse of the soul, when in the light of conscience it sees itself in its sin, is to hide from the face of God in the shadow of the trees, like Adam and Eve in the garden of Eden, when they saw their nakedness. Calm self-complacency and proud self-satisfaction disappear and are replaced by shame, confusion, and even fear at the things that have been revealed to man about himself. This is a difficult and dangerous 'hour before daybreak' because usually at this point cowardly depression and profound disappointment in ourselves lie in wait for us. The force of repentance draws us, however, not to a passive contemplation of sin, but to active struggle against it. Repentance forces us to seek deliverance from sin, purification: 'Make me a clean heart, O God; and renew a right spirit within me', prays the soul together with the Psalmist.[2]

At this point the work of penitence begins, apart from which salvation cannot be attained; it begins but it has no end, for it is life-long. Without this work there is no active penitence but only a vague wish for it. And this is the second door of repentance. Woe to us if we confine ourselves to the knowledge of sin and, refusing the effort, avoid direct struggle against it; such a man 'has no cloke for his sin' (John 15.22). But self-knowledge leads to self-reproach, and self-reproach to fresh self-knowledge; the depths of the heart are open more and more, new sins come to memory, and at the very bottom the serpent of original sin writhes its coils. Spiritual labour united with self-scrutiny does not, however, lead to weakness or depression, but strengthens one's courage, renews the powers

[1] Sung on the Wednesday evening of the fifth week of Lent, and in parts on the first four days of Lent—a kind of scriptural anthology of penitence. It consists of 250 hymns. St Andrew lived 660–740. [Ed.]
[2] Psalm 51.10.

of the soul, and is like salt for it. A penitent goes on working away, unobserved, in a state of spiritual alertness which is reflected in his whole life. And he has his solace, for the heavenly Father gives him bounties in the sacrament of penance, gives him the joy of forgiveness. 'Restore unto me the joy of thy salvation, and uphold me with thy free spirit', the penitent soul repeats with the Psalmist.[1] The work of penitence is the heart of all works, and this is why in great ascetics it is accompanied by a gracious blossoming of all their spiritual powers. Through penitence the nature of man as originally created is liberated from the distortions of sin. It was in order to manifest to sinners the salutary fruits of penitence that the Lord granted the remission of sins in the sacrament of penance. Through it the past becomes nonexistent, the stripes of sin are healed by the power of Christ. But only that which has been found by man in his own heart, condemned, and fought against, can be thus wiped out. Man must himself open the sad pages in his book of life that they may be deleted through the grace of the sacrament; unrepented sins are not wiped out. True penitence is useful in every way; it gives healing and health, peace and joy, humility and courage, sobriety and watchfulness. Through enmity to sin it strengthens our love for God and testifies to it. We need the power of penitence at all times, but the holy Church has singled out and blessed the days of Lent as a special season for it. And, behold, now our souls are called to it by the prayer, 'Open to me the doors of penitence, O Life-giver.'

[1] Psalm 51.12.

Divine Gladness

Come . . . partake of the divine gladness . . . of the
Kingdom of Christ.

Easter canon

On Easter eve, when the procession, having processed round
the church, stops in front of the closed doors, the minds of the
faithful pass through an incalculably brief but spiritually
significant moment as it were of perplexed, questioning silence:
'Who shall roll us away the stone from the door of the
sepulchre?'[1] Will the sepulchre be empty because Christ is
risen? When the doors open at the sign of the cross and we
enter the brilliantly illuminated church to the singing of the
triumphant Easter hymn, our hearts overflow with joy because
Christ is risen from the dead, and the Easter miracle takes
place in our souls. For we 'see Christ's resurrection'; 'cleansing
our senses', we behold 'Christ shining with light' and
'approaching as like a Bridegroom He comes forth from the
tomb'. We lose consciousness of time and place, transcend the
confines of ourselves, and enter the timeless sabbath of 'rest
to the people of God'.[2]

Earthly colours fade in the radiance of the white ray of
Easter, and the soul contemplates only 'the unapproachable
light of resurrection': 'Today all is filled with light, the heavens
and the earth and the nether world.' On Easter eve it is
given to man to anticipate the life of the world to come, to
enter the kingdom of glory, the kingdom of God. We have
no words to express the revelation of the Easter vigil, for it
is a mystery of the age to come, 'the language of which is
silence'.

The perfect joy given us on that night, in accordance with
the Lord's promise, is the Holy Spirit, who by the will of the
Father reveals to us the risen Christ. The Holy Spirit is the
actual joy of the Holy Trinity, the Father's joy in the Son and
the Son's in the Father, and he is our joy in Christ's resur-

[1] Mark 16.3.   [2] Heb. 4.9–10.

rection. In and through him we see the risen Christ, and in us
he is the light of Christ's resurrection. Easter is for us not one
among other holidays, but 'the feast of feasts and triumph of
triumphs'. All the twelve great holidays[1] give us knowledge
of the kingdom of God as manifested in his works in this
world. But Easter is not a commemoration of a past event, it
is a part of the world to come. Easter is an anticipation on
the earth of the manifested glory for which Christ prayed to
the Father in his high-priestly prayer—of the heavenly
Jerusalem which in the fullness of time comes down from
heaven to earth, according to the prophet's vision: 'Arise,
shine, O New Jerusalem, for the glory of the Lord is risen
upon thee.'[2] Easter is eternal life consisting in the knowledge
of and communion with God. It is righteousness, peace, and
joy in the Holy Spirit. The first word of the risen Lord to the
women was 'rejoice'[3] and to the apostles 'Peace be unto
you'.[4]

The life of the world to come is not mere negation or
destruction of this world, but the perpetuation of everything
in it that is worthy of being preserved, just as eternity is not
oblivion or annihilation of time but a cessation of its changeable course. In the resurrection the glorification of the creature
is accomplished by the power of God, but in its own life it is
through the work of self-renunciation. Christ's resurrection
takes place in virtue of his voluntary suffering and death on
the cross: 'having overcome death by death'. The victory
over death is attained from within, by death itself. The life
of this world is lived out to the end in the self-abasement of
Christ's death, and death, experienced and tasted to the end,
has no more power to hold him (Acts 2.24), for it itself dies in
him. 'O death, where is thy sting?'[5] 'Death is swallowed up in
victory.' Resurrection is not the creation of a new life, but
victory over death itself, the dawn of eternal life springing

[1] These are: Christmas, Epiphany, Candlemas, Lady Day, Palm
Sunday, Ascension Day, Whit Sunday (Trinity Sunday), the Transfiguration, Holy Cross Day, and Our Lady's Birthday, Presentation,
and Falling Asleep. [Ed.]

[2] Isa. 60.1.
[3] Matt. 28.9 (in English versions 'All hail').
[4] Luke 24.86; John 20.19, 26.
[5] 1 Cor. 15.55.

up from death, 'Christ coming forth from the tomb like a bridegroom'. Christ's resurrection is therefore the continuation of
his saving death which crowns his redeeming passion and the
whole path of the Incarnation. Christ's resurrection is bound
up with the cross, for it is achieved through it, by the sacrificial power of love and obedience. 'We worship Thy Cross,
O Lord, and sing and glorify Thy resurrection.' In the overcoming of death, in the victory of resurrection, the cross is
the basis and the force of Easter joy.

The bliss of paradise preserves the memory of past suffering
overcome and suffused with light, just as light itself is the
victory over 'the abyss of darkness', and as God's world is the
cloak of beauty and harmony thrown over the 'earth without
form and void'. This world is preserved through being transformed into its future state and is transfigured, as the earthly
body of the Lord Jesus was transfigured in the resurrection.
The body of the risen Lord preserves the wounds of the nails
and the pierced side as the testimony to its identity; in this
unity of the life of this and of the future world is the force of
Christ's resurrection made manifest.

The image of resurrection is inscribed in nature, and its
token is the springtime resurrection. After the winter torpor
the spring brings forth new growth from the earth, new green
spikes emerge and are filled with the sap of life. The spring
decks itself with the multi-coloured raiment of resurrection
under the vivifying rays of the sun. Every spring prophesies
the spring that is to come for the world as a whole. The death
of nature is overcome by the warmth of life, and the Easter
of nature gives place to the Christian Easter. Just as winter
leads us along its hard path to spring, so in Christian life the
days of Lent and of Holy Week bring us to Holy Easter.
Sometimes people want to avoid this path, to escape the
knowledge and experience of Holy Week. But then their
senses remain closed, there is no light burning in their hearts
to light the Easter candle. For 'yesterday I was crucified and
buried with Thee, today I rise again with Thee, O Risen Lord'.
Blessed is he who can repeat these words of the Easter hymn
in his heart. Joy is the crowning of sorrow; a great light shines
in the darkness and the shadow of death, death is overcome by
death, and the Easter triumph is the spiritual fruit of the

sorrow and the hardships of Lent. After the sorrow of winter the Bridegroom calls his bride: 'Rise up, my love, my fair one, and come away.'[1]

The rays of Christ's light penetrate the whole universe. In that light the departed are living for us, and we send them the greetings of Easter, the message of resurrection which they know in their own way. Not only rational and animate creatures feel the force of the resurrection, but the world as a whole rises in the body of Christ, rejoicing with Paschal joy. 'Let the heavens triumph and the whole earth be glad and all the world, visible and invisible, rejoice.' The eyes of a seer clearly behold in nature the play of Paschal joy: the sun 'gambols', the air and water and plants are illumined by the rays of divine gladness. The rising human spirit cannot bear to see deathlike, lifeless nature and calls it also to share in Christ's resurrection.

Easter is Eucharistic joy. The Lord has not parted from us in his Ascension but left us Holy Communion as a bond with him. Partaking of the heavenly bread and the cup of life, we tangibly feel the manifested Christ and magnify him with the resurrection hymn: 'O thou great Passover and hallowed above all, O Christ! O Thou the wisdom and the Word and Power of God! Grant that we may partake of Thee more truly, in that day of Thy kingdom which shall have no end.' The feast of Easter already is that day, and Paschal joy is akin to the joy of our Communion. The faithful are filled with Christ, the Lord is near to us, he appears to us as he appeared to the apostles before Ascension. Easter is a special sacrament given to the Church by the Holy Spirit so that the believers may know the risen Lord: 'Having seen Christ's resurrection, let us worship the Lord Jesus.'

Easter is joy about the Church; in virtue of it we find ourselves within the Church, in the one life of one body, the body of Christ. That which usually remains only a call and a promise appears now before us as highest reality. Joy in the Church enables us to see one another in God and, through this, to rejoice in our neighbour as a lover rejoices in the beloved. Easter fills us with the Holy Spirit who is the joy of love. This gift is granted to spiritual men as the crown of their ascetic

[1] Song of Songs 2.10.

achievement. Easter was always shining in St Seraphim's heart, and he met those who came to him with words of Paschal greeting: 'Christ is risen, my joy.' And on this night we too, reserved, gloomy, and sullen as we are, have our hearts open to the triumphant joy of love and greet one another with the Easter kiss and the gracious words, 'Christ is risen'. Personal injuries, bad feelings melt away in this light. Can those who love fail to forgive, and is not forgiveness the highest joy of love? It likens us to God, who forgives the prodigal son and crowns him in a marriage feast. Easter is universal forgiveness in the joy of love. In Paschal love we apprehend the love of God which passes all understanding. Its light leaves no room for darkness or shadow. All is melted and forged together in its fire. 'The day of resurrection! Let us shine with its triumph and embrace one another. Let us say "Brothers" and through the resurrection forgive all to those who hate us.' Our hearts are aflame with the joy of love, as were the hearts of the two disciples when they saw and heard him journeying with them. Behold now too he is among us, seen invisibly. Amen.

Pentecost and the Descent of the Spirit

The Lord has created man in his image in order to have him for his friend, to let him participate in the divine life, and by dwelling in him to make him a god through grace. When man fell and deviated from his destined purpose, the Son of God assumed human nature and, having redeemed human sin, restored to man the possibility he had lost. In and through him divine nature was completely united to the human. But Christ's work of redemption had to bear fruit in salvation and be realized in a new life in which man was to participate through receiving the life-giving Holy Spirit. When Christ ascended from the world—in which, however, he remains perpetually as the perfect God-man—the Holy Spirit was to descend upon the world. The descent of the Holy Spirit is directly connected with the Incarnation; indeed it may be said to be the purpose of it, as Christ explains to his disciples: 'It is expedient for you that I go unto the Father' in order to send the Holy Spirit and baptize the disciples with fire. Christ's incarnation unites us to him and is a firm basis of our participation in the divine life; but only if we receive the Holy Spirit can this life be realized in us, and the union and inter-penetration of the human and the divine be mysteriously and inexpressibly manifested.

The word 'inspiration' in the human sense means a state in which man is conscious of the presence in him of some new power, proceeding as it were from his higher self; without losing his identity he feels he is a different person, discovering new, unexplored possibilities within himself. But this inspira-tion, revealing to man the hidden or dormant powers of his own spirit, is only an image of that which happens when man receives the Spirit of God and is penetrated by it and deified, thus becoming one with Christ who lives in him. The descent of the Holy Spirit is the fulfilment of Christ's work and the realization of God's conception of man, since man was created to be the temple of the Holy Spirit together with the world of nature of which he is meant to be the head and the soul.

The cosmic Pentecost in 'the upper room' at Jerusalem had been anticipated and prepared from the foundation of the world which has always been vivified by the Holy Spirit. At the first moment of creation when the void and formless earth was called into being 'the Spirit of God moved upon the face of the waters', and this was the first cosmic Pentecost by anticipation. The second, human Pentecost took place when God in creating man 'breathed into his nostrils the breath of life'.[1] According to the testimony of the Church, 'every soul is vivified by the Holy Spirit'. As first created, man was a spirit-bearer, although he lost his gifts in consequence of the Fall. But even in his fallen state he was not altogether deprived of the grace of God's Spirit. It is given him through his natural spiritual powers, for the original divine image in him is not lost but only dimmed. And by special divine dispensation the gracious gifts of the Holy Spirit were given to man in the chosen flock, in the Old Testament Church through different ministrations—through the ministrations of priests, elders, kings, prophets, warriors, artists. The life of the Old Testament Church is full of manifestations of grace. And yet the break between God and man could not be overcome before the coming of Christ; the Holy Spirit's gracious gifts brightened man, so to speak, from without but could not penetrate into his being and make him a temple of the Holy Spirit.

But as man ascended, nurtured by grace, he was gradually made ready to receive God, and a time came at last when there appeared on earth a being capable of receiving the Holy Spirit and becoming the temple of God—the Immaculate Virgin. The Holy Spirit descended upon her at the Incarnation, and this was the Pentecost of the Mother of God. It gave the Virgin Mary the power to become the Mother of the Lord, but it still left the possibility for the Immaculate Virgin herself to take part in all humanity's Pentecost at Jerusalem.

The human nature of the Lord Jesus Christ knew its Pentecost when he was baptized, and the Holy Spirit

[1] Genesis 2.7.

descended like a dove and lighted upon him; this descent of the Spirit upon the new Adam already contained the substance of the universal Pentecost to come. But it could not come until the redeeming sacrifice was completed and Christ's human nature was glorified through his Ascension and his sitting at the right hand of the Father. Only when the Son of Man had finally deified and glorified the whole of his human nature did he send the Holy Spirit from the heavenly Father unto the whole of mankind—just as the Holy Spirit abiding in him was sent to light upon his human nature. This was Christ's last promise to the apostles before the Ascension, expressing the whole purpose of his work: 'Wait for the promise of the Father . . . ye shall be baptized with the Holy Ghost.'[1]

The descent of the Holy Spirit was an event that happened at a particular time and place. St Luke describes it in the Acts of the Apostles: 'And suddenly there came a sound from heaven as of a rushing mighty wind . . . and there appeared unto them cloven tongues like as of fire, and it sat upon each of them. And they were all filled with the Holy Ghost.'[2] The descent of the Holy Spirit took place in a way perceptible to all and indeed actually visible; and its effect was equally perceptible to those who had received him. They felt themselves to be new men and acquired the gift of speaking with other tongues. At the building of the tower of Babel which marked the utmost limit of man's falling away from God and opposing him, the division of tongues took place, in accordance with God's will; at Pentecost that division was healed. The Holy Spirit unites all tongues in the Church, for in Christ there is neither Greek nor Jew. Each apostle received a separate tongue of the one Holy Spirit, for as St Paul says: 'Now there are diversities of gifts . . . and there are differences of administrations . . . and there are diversities of operations but the same Spirit, and the manifestation of the spirit is given to every man to profit withal.'[3] In the early Church the gifts of the Holy Spirit were so abundant that some of them were coveted more than others, as described by St Paul in 1 Corinthians 12–14.

The descent of the Holy Spirit with the laying on of

[1] Acts 1.4–5.   [2] Acts 2.2–3.   [3] 1 Cor. 12.4–7.

the apostles' hands was always perceptible, as can be seen from various instances: of the Samaritans (Acts 8.15–17), the Ethiopian Eunuch (8.39), Cornelius (10.44–7), and the Ephesians (19.2–6). In the subsequent life of the Church, as in our own day, these gifts are no longer always perceptible, owing to our sinful frailty and through a special dispensation of Providence; but their power and actuality are not affected thereby. The tongues of fire that descended upon the world at Pentecost remain with us, and we, Christians, live by the active power of Pentecost, for it abides in the Church of Christ. All that takes place in the Church—sacraments, prayers, holy rites—is a manifestation of the Pentecostal tongues of fire abiding in the world. The holiness of the Church, its spiritual gifts and achievements, are all due to the power of Pentecost. At the heights of holiness the fiery tongues of Pentecost become perceptible among us too: the face of St Seraphim of Sarov[1] shone like the sun when he manifested the presence of the Holy Spirit to Motovilov. And even now people's eyes shine at moments of prayerful rapture, clearly testifying to the Holy Spirit resting upon them.

It is given to every one of us to have a part in Pentecost, but we must nurture this gift and acquire it through labour and effort. Continuing both visibly and invisibly, Pentecost goes on doing its work in the world and in mankind. The Holy Spirit living in the Church builds up in it the Body of Christ, the kingdom of saints awaiting the glory to come. Not only man but nature as a whole is predestined for that glory. The Israelites made tabernacles of branches at the feast of Pentecost, and now Christians bring into church flowers, grasses, and branches of trees. In this way the whole of nature enters the upper room in Jerusalem and has a part in the feast of Pentecost. As St Paul says, the whole creation is waiting for the manifestation of the glory of the sons of God, for the new heaven and a new earth, for the cosmic Pentecost beyond the threshold of universal resurrection. The Holy Spirit who now lives in the Church and makes it a kingdom of grace shall make it the kingdom of glory; the image of God shall be reflected in all creation and God shall be all in all. But this future kingdom of glory will be the fulfilment of what has

[1] St Seraphim died in 1833. [Ed.]

already been achieved through the work of Christ and the descent of the Holy Spirit into the world. The Lord is already united to his creation. He has deified it and abides in it. We call the day of Pentecost 'the day of the Holy Trinity', as it were, a second Epiphany. God the Father manifested in his Son manifests himself also in the Spirit who proceeds from the Father and is sent by the Son. God is tri-personal love, mutual love between the three divine Persons and love for the creature manifested in the descent of the Spirit. And now this divine condescension is revealed to the end: the Lord has both created the world and come to dwell in it—the Father through the Son and the Holy Spirit. Amen.

The Exceeding Glory

'For He received from God the Father honour and glory, when there came such a voice to Him from the excellent glory, This is my beloved Son, in whom I am well pleased.'[1]

The day of Transfiguration (6 August) stands as it were outside the general order of the Lord's feasts which correspond to the successive events of Christ's earthly life. It seems as though the date for it had been selected arbitrarily, to fit in with the blessing of fruits. But this of course is not essentially connected with the feast. A more profound meaning of the feast being, so to speak, detached from others may be found in the fact that the actual event of the Transfiguration in its inner significance points to the life of the world to come, outside our temporal order. It speaks of the kingdom of glory, of the transfiguration of the world to which it bears witness in anticipation, revealing it as seen from here. 'Master, it is good for us to be here'[2]—such was the involuntary testimony of St Peter in the presence of this vision of 'the Kingdom of God come with power'.[3] He wanted to retain that which did not really belong to this age, though it happened in it. Only after the Lord's coming in glory 'shall we ever be with the Lord'.[4] But here, on Mount Tabor, the marvellous vision faded away, and coming down from the mount of Transfiguration the apostles found themselves once more in the unenlightened realm of the prince of this world, among the possessed, the sick, and those of little faith.

The Lord's Transfiguration bears witness to the glory of the world to come, revealed in the *parousia*.[5] And yet it is included in the texture of gospel events and of the earthly ministry of the Lord Jesus. Attentive reading of the gospel convinces us that the Transfiguration was a dividing line in his life, just as his appearance to the world after the baptism was. The latter,

[1] 2 Peter 1.17.　　[2] Mark 9.5.　　[3] Mark 9.1.　　[4] 1 Thess. 4.17.
[5] Greek for the glorious appearing of our Lord at his second coming.

in its human aspect, expresses Christ's formed will to fulfil his mission and is, as it were, a consecration for it. The former expresses his formed will to suffer, to go into Jerusalem to be crucified. The Lord had for some time been more and more definitely preparing his disciples, who from human frailty were resisting this salutary will. The fact of the Transfiguration is a part of that preparation: 'So that when they see Thee crucified, they understand Thy voluntary suffering'. But Christ's glory revealed in the Transfiguration testifies to his final glory which is already attained in anticipation through his willingness to suffer.

When at the Last Supper the Lord mystically enacts with the disciples his impending death on the cross, he also testifies in anticipation to his glory to come. Events cast their light from the future into the past and the present, already pregnant with that future. And it is in this sense that before his passion the Lord speaks of glory: 'Now is the Son of man glorified, and God is glorified in Him' (John 13.31). Similarly, still earlier, on the Mount of Transfiguration, Moses and Elijah, coming from the world beyond the grave and also illumined by the anticipation of the glory to come, spoke with him of his decease which he should accomplish at Jerusalem. The Father accepts the Son's will to suffer and sends 'exceeding glory' overshadowing him as a bright cloud. At the Lord's baptism, when the Holy Spirit descended upon him, the Father's voice came from heaven, adopting him: 'This is my beloved Son, in whom I am well pleased';[1] the same voice was also heard from 'the cloud of glory' at the Transfiguration, i.e. at another manifestation of the power of the Holy Spirit. Similarly, before Christ's passion the Father's voice came from heaven declaring his future glorification: 'I have both glorified it and will glorify it again.'[2] The Father crowns with glory the Son's sacrificial will and confirms it as it were by a fresh act of adoption. The Lord's Transfiguration understood in this sense is a spiritually pre-accomplished self-immolation of the Son in accordance with the Father's will—the filial 'Thy will be done'.

But what was the new reality, never seen in the world before, made manifest on Mount Tabor? What was it that the

[1] Matt. 3.17.   [2] John 12.28.

mountain, and the air, and the sky, and the earth, and the whole world, and Christ's disciples saw? What was the glory that shone round about the apostles? It was a clear manifestation of the Holy Spirit resting upon Chirist and in him transfiguring the creation. It was an anticipatory revelation of 'a new heaven and a new earth'—of the world transfigured and illumined by beauty. Like Epiphany, it was a revelation of the Holy Trinity as a whole—of the Father sending his Spirit upon his beloved Son and in him upon all creation, to which Christ united himself by assuming human nature. It was a revelation of that which can only happen after Christ's resurrection and the universal resurrection to come. The kingdom of God is foretold not in words only, but in deeds. The light of Mount Tabor was truly a divine light and not merely a visual and as it were illusory impression on the part of the apostles. It was the light of the Holy Spirit overshadowing the creature, which has been seen and made manifest by some of God's elect—spiritual men, certain hermits on Mount Athos, St Simeon the New Theologian, and St Seraphim of Sarov almost in our own day. They too lit their tapers at the Tabor light of the Transfiguration. The Church has given special attention to the elucidation of this truth. Its preliminary dogmatic exposition was defined in the fourteenth century, in connection with the so-called Palamite disputes (in the Church of Constantinople). Indirectly the dogma about the light of Mount Tabor being a true manifestation of the Deity testifies to the power of the Lord's Transfiguration which revealed to men 'the ever-abiding light' of God (the *troparion* of the feast of Transfiguration). This dogmatic definition contains not only the particular assertion that in the Lord's Transfiguration the disciples beheld the true radiance of the Deity, but also a more general truth that the light of the Transfiguration has already penetrated into the world and abides in it. The world's transfiguration has been anticipated in virtue of Christ's Incarnation and the Pentecost of the Holy Spirit.

The Holy Spirit acts now in the world through grace which is to be found in the whole life of the Church and in its mysterious gifts. But he is also present in the world as glory, which to the end of this age remains hidden, but in accordance with God's will reveals itself even now to God's elect, just as the light of the Transfiguration was revealed to the three apostles chosen by Christ for the purpose—Peter, James, and John. The Holy Spirit has descended upon the world, and the world has already been glorified, though this is not as yet made manifest. But for the elect this true future image of the world already shines like lightning in the light of Mount Tabor. The world appears to them as transfigured.

But what does 'transfiguration' mean? Does it mean that the old image is cancelled, or that it is truly revealed in glory, in the all-subduing—because it is all-convincing—manifestation of beauty? 'It is good to be here'—'very good'. This is how the world is created by the divine Providence, though it is not as yet revealed to human contemplation. And yet on Mount Tabor it is revealed already. And this contemplation of the incorruptible, archetypal beauty is the joy of joys, 'the perfect joy'. This is why the feast of Transfiguration is an anticipation of joy, the feast of beauty. Beauty does not yet reign in this world, though it has been enthroned in it through the divine Incarnation and Pentecost. It follows Christ on the way to the cross; in the world beauty is crucified. It is sacrificial beauty, and the words about 'going forth to suffer' are said in reference to it. Yet it is beauty. And it is the feast of this sacrificial beauty that we celebrate on the day of our Lord's Transfiguration.

'May Thine everlasting light shine also upon us sinners.' Amen.

Bibliography

Principal works by Sergius Bulgakov, arranged according to date of publication. All are in Russian unless otherwise indicated.

1896 *The Role of the Market in Capitalist Production* (Moscow)

1901 *Capitalism and Agriculture* (Moscow)

1903 *From Marxism to Idealism* (Moscow)

1911 *Two Cities* (Moscow)

1912 *The Philosophy of Economics* (Moscow)

1917 *The Unfading Light* (Moscow)

1918 *Quiet Thoughts* (Moscow)

1926 *St Peter and St John* (Paris)

1927 *The Burning Bush* (Paris)
     The Friend of the Bridegroom (Paris)
     The Tragedy of Philosophy (Darmstadt). In German.

1929 *Karl Marx as a Religious Type* (Warsaw)
     Jacob's Ladder (Paris)

1931 *Ikons* (Paris)

1933 *The Lamb of God* (Paris)

1935 *The Orthodox Church* (London). In English.

1936 *The Comforter* (Paris)

1937 *The Wisdom of God* (London). In English.

1945 *The Bride of the Lamb* (Paris)

1946 *Autobiographical Notes* (Paris)

1948 *The Apocalypse of John* (Paris)

1953 *Philosophy of the Name* (Paris)

1955 *Life from the Tomb* (Paris)

1959 *The Vatican Dogma* (South Canaan, Pa.). In English.

1961 *Dialogue Between God and Man* (Marbourg)

1965 *Orthodoxy* (Paris)

1973 *Spiritual Journal* (Paris)

www.ingramcontent.com/pod-product-compliance
Lightning Source LLC
Chambersburg PA
CBHW060313100426
42812CB00003B/769